SUPER POWERS OF THE MIND

Cody Jones

SUPER POWERS OF THE MIND

Transform Your Life
Through the Twelve Powers

Cody L. Jones, DVM

QUINTEN PUBLISHING

Commerce Twp, Michigan

Library of Congress Cataloging-in-Publication Data

Jones, Cody L. (Cody Luther), 1949-
    Super powers of the mind : transform your life through the twelve powers / Cody L. Jones.
        p.   cm.
    Includes index.
    ISBN 1-878040-07-3 : $12.00
    1. Spiritual life. I. Title.
BL624.J6475 1993
248.4--dc20   92-34528
                                  CIP

First printing, April 1993

Printed in the United States of America

This book is dedicated to **Jack Boland,**
my beloved teacher, minister, and way-shower

and

to my best friend and partner in life

- Janice Marie Jones

Did You Borrow This Book?

Want a Copy of Your Own?

Need a Great Gift for a Friend or Loved One?

Your local library or bookstore
will be delighted to order your copy
from America's leading wholesaler of books:

BAKER & TAYLOR BOOKS

ACKNOWLEDGMENTS

Through the past seven years of research and writing, I have had the great fortune to attend many outstanding classes and seminars at the **Church of Today** in Warren Michigan presented by some of the world's most creative, inspiring, dedicated, and capable individuals. They have contributed greatly to my spiritual growth and understanding and include:

Gregory Barrette	Mike Matoin
Mary Boggs	Peter McWilliams
Jack Boland	Grace Merrick
Karen Boland	Vrle Minto
Leo Booth	Michael Murphy
Les Brown	Al & Jan Mustin
Depok Chopra	Ralph Nichols
Alan Cohen	Patricia Olds
Don & Judy Crooks	Mary Omwake
Tom Crumb	Pete Paris
Peter Daniels	Freddie Paris
Giles Desjardins	Norman Peale
Lillian Desjardins	Paul Pearsal
Linda Dominic	Della Reese
Wayne Dyer	Ray Santerini
White Eagle	Robert Schuller
Famous Amos	Ron & Lenore Scott
Sonya Friedman	Bernie Siegel
Charles Garfield	Don Sizer
Larry Gatlin	Michael Smith
Jack Graf	Susan Smith-Jones
Carolyn Grezecki	W Clement Stone
Ralph Grezecki	Diane Szymanski
Bob & Jane Handley	Don Tocco
Mark Hansen	Bob Trask
Charly Heavenrich	Dean Tucker
Patricia M Holl	Denis Waitley
Susan Jeffers	Brian Weiss
Earnie Larsen	Terri Whitaker
David Lindsey	Mike Wickett
Guy Lynch	Don & Judy Crooks
Og Mandino	Gary Zukav

CONTENTS

PREFACE

In 1968, I was 19 years old and confined to bed and ice chips for a week following my belated tonsillectomy. Having just received a shiny red new King James Bible with bright gold edges, I eagerly leapt into reading what I had heard was the world's greatest classic on higher consciousness and positive living.

With great dismay, I found myself drop kicked out of the Garden, murdered by Cain, and drowned in the Flood. My birthright was stolen by my twin brother and I was sold into slavery. After escaping from the Egyptians, I massacred the Canaanites and joined Job in his depression. Finally, I was swallowed by a great fish and vomited onto a beach.

Fortunately the week was up and I never read the Bible again for sixteen years. Then in 1984, God knocked on my hood. My Veterinary practice was struggling, my wife was chronically sick and housebound, and my car stuck four feet in the air and died.

Seeking help I turned to God and my life began to turn around. I learned to see beyond shortcomings of characters in the Bible and to recognize universal wisdom and spiritual principles taught by the Bible. As I applied this ancient wisdom to my life, things got better! After two years my business doubled, my wife was healthy, I owned a shiny new sports car, and we took a three week vacation cruise to China and stood on the Great Wall.

In view of God's great bounty, I knew I had to do something significant in return. I spent the next seven years researching success principles from the Bible so that others could recognize and benefit from them too! This book is the result.

The time you spend on your spiritual growth is a great investment in your future. Good luck on your odyssey. May the white light of peace, health, joy, love, happiness, abundance, prosperity, fun and success be with you always!

CODY L. JONES, DVM
Easter, 1993

GOD IS

God is

the reality of my being.

He is my Life, my Mind and Spirit,

the animating Principle,

my Creator,

and the Substance

and Soul of my being.

God is

a loving presence

in the midst of me,

closer than breathing,

and is found

in the stillness of my being,

when thought is tranquil.

TRANSFORMATION

Create for yourself the full, beautiful life for which your heart yearns. Within you lies a wonderful potential ready to blossom forth. The life God has given you is a precious gift. A fountain of miraculous demonstrations springs up around the spiritual principles given to you in the greatest book of all time - the Bible.

Jesus came that you might have life, and have it abundantly. He invites you to move beyond a routine, fearful, and limited existence into a dynamic abundant life. You live this abundant life by daring to discover your spiritual identity.

As you work with these ideas, changes will appear in little ways. A co-worker you once had difficulty with may offer you a pleasant compliment. A business transaction may unfold in an unusually successful way. Your days will begin to seem fuller, happier and more productive. You will notice more harmony in all your relationships. Prosperity will enter your affairs. You will start to feel healthier and take on a new zest

and vitality for life. At first, these
changes may seem coincidental. They are
not. They are a result of your increased
awareness and commitment to living a
spiritual life.

Jesus promises you,"He who believes
in me, will also do the works that I do;
and greater things than these will he
do." Now is the time to accept Jesus'
invitation and open your eyes to new
possibilities for living.

Did you know that you are a trinity?
The trinity of God is Father, Son, and
Holy Ghost. The trinity of you is body,
mind, and spirit. Your "I AM" spirit is
the spirit of God within you - also
called the Christ Spirit and Holy Spirit.
Your mind (thoughts and feelings) is your
soul. When you repent (change your
thoughts and feelings) and align your
soul with God, you enter the Kingdom of
God. Your thoughts and feelings sprout
spiritual wings that help you rise above
material limitations. Your mind mounts
up with wings as eagles to express your
Christ nature.

This book is your opportunity to
transform your life through the Holy
Spirit (the whole spirit of God). In
Psalms, David prayed, "Create in me a
clean heart, O God, and put a new and
right spirit within me" (Ps 51:10). When
Jesus appeared to the disciples after his
resurrection, he breathed on them and
said, "Receive the Holy Spirit" (John
20:22). **Today is your day to receive the
Holy Spirit!**

And when Jesus was baptized,

he went up
immediately from the water,
and behold,

the heavens were opened

and he saw
the Spirit of God
descending like a dove,
and alighting on him;

and lo,
a voice from heaven,
saying,

"This is my beloved Son,
with whom
I am well pleased."
Matthew 3:16-17

SAY "YES!" TO YOUR DREAMS

At the end of each chapter are affirmations. Everything you want or need is trying to happen to you - and it will begin happening to you the moment you learn to say "yes!" to things and conditions that have not yet become reality. Affirmations are vehicles you can use to help you arrive at a "yes!" position in your life.

An affirmation is a positive declaration (usually aloud) that a fact or idea is so. You can use that concept to influence your own thoughts and feelings and, therefore... your life. You can "affirm" the existence of positive qualities about yourself and positive facts about your life - despite possible evidence to the contrary.

Affirmations have the power to bring about dramatic changes in your life. But you must believe that affirmations work. Affirmations represent the truth of your inner Higher Being (so they aren't necessarily statements of outer "fact" at a given moment). They inspire and moti-vate you when stated (and repeated) with the same intensity of feeling you would have if you knew the affirmations were true.

SYMBOLS OF THE SUPER POWERS

POWER	OLD & NEW TESTAMENT COLOR & STONE	
Faith	Abraham	Peter
	Dark Blue	Jasper
Strength	Samson	Andrew
	Spring Green	Sapphire
Wisdom	Solomon	James Z
	Yellow	Agate
Love	David	John
	Pink	Emerald
Power	Elijah	Phillip
	Purple	Onyx
Imagination	Joseph	Nathanael
	Light Blue	Carnelian
Understanding	Daniel	Thomas
	Gold	Chrysolite
Will	Joshua	Matthew
	Silver	Beryl
Order	Elisha	James A
	Olive Green	Topaz
Zeal	Jacob	Simon Z
	Orange	Chrysoprase
Renunciation	Moses	Thaddaeus
	Russet	Jacinth
Life	Noah	Matthias
	Red	Amethyst

STONES AND COLORS

Stones - The twelve stones of the New
Jerusalem (Revelation 21:19-20)
symbolize your Twelve Powers
in a similar manner that your
birthstone symbolizes your
birthday. When you wear one of
the symbolic stones, it can
remind you of its associated
Super Power within you.

Colors - The colors for the Twelve Powers
evolved from traditional color
associations:

Faith .....   Dark Blue..True blue faith
Strength ..   Spring Green....Relaxation
Wisdom ....   Yellow...Sunshine and light
Love .....   Pink........Valentine's Day
Power .....   Purple.......Color of kings
Imagination   Light Blue......Blueprints
Understanding Gold......Gift of wise men
Will ......   Silver...The silver lining
Order .....   Olive Green....Color of $$$
Zeal ......   Orange...Stimulating color
Renunciation   Russet......Autumn leaves
Life ....   Red.....Color of Christmas

FAITH

I go to meet my good!

WHAT IS FAITH?

Faith is my confident belief that God's mighty power is actively at work in every area of my life. With faith I can meet and overcome all obstacles and achieve self-mastery. I turn my life around by turning my thinking around. Persistent, positive thinking attracts opportunities where none seemed possible.

As I remind myself that God is in charge, I transform feelings of anxiety into feelings of excitement. I trust God's spirit working in and through me and other people. As I place my trust in God, my life is enriched.

I alter my world by changing my perceptions. I rejoice in knowing that my way is clear, my future blessed. As I take one day at a time, God's ever present activity within and around me unites me with my good. God goes before me and makes the crooked way straight.

SYMBOLS OF FAITH

Old Testament - Abraham

Through faith Abraham broke from pagan idolatry and committed to a belief in only one God. He followed his God to a new land promised to his descendants.

New Testament - Peter

Peter's faith solidified following Jesus' postresurrection appearance and threefold commission to shepherd the flock of God. He spoke for the apostles on the day of Pentecost with great inspiration and effect.

He was the first of the apostles to perform a miracle in the name of Jesus - healing a cripple at the Beautiful Gate of the Temple. Peter also healed Aeneas, the paralytic at Lydda, and he raised to life Dorcas, a woman of many good works in Joppa.

Color - Dark Blue
Stone - Green Jasper

YOU'LL SEE IT

WHEN YOU BELIEVE IT!

****

He who believes in me
will also do the works
that I do;
and greater works than these
will he do.
John 14:12

Believe in the Lord your God,
and you shall have success!
2 Chronicles 20:20
(Living Bible)

All things are possible
to him who believes.
Mark 9:23

Faith is the assurance of things hoped for,
the conviction of things not seen.
Hebrews 11:1

A woman who had been sick
for twelve years with internal bleeding
came up behind Him
and touched a tassel of His robe.

For she thought,
"If I only touch Him,
I will be healed."

Jesus turned around and spoke to her.
"Daughter," he said, "all is well!
Your faith has healed you."
And the woman was well from that moment.
Matthew 9:20-22
(Living Bible)

We are always of good courage...
for we walk by faith,
not by sight.
2 Corinthians 5:6-7

"Lord, if it is you, bid me come to you
on the water." He said, "Come." So
Peter got out of the boat and walked on
the water and came to Jesus.
Matthew 14:28-29

In God I trust.
Psalms 56:4

TRUST

During my freshman year at Cornell University, I was on ROTC Army scholarship and signed up with their elite special forces called "Rangers." At 6 AM one sunny morning we assembled in Barton Hall to learn the art of rappelling. Climbing to the top of the bleachers, we quickly mastered the technique of sliding down a rope along a 30 foot drop.

I was feeling quite confident with my ability until I was led to a local gorge. I felt goose bumps run up my back as I peered over the cliff's edge to the stream lined with jagged rocks 200 foot below. As we used to say back home, one mistake here and I would "buy the farm."

As the leader was rappelling over the edge, I noticed that the rope seemed a bit frayed where it rubbed against the rocky edge. With my heart in my mouth I faced my fear and put my trust and confidence in God. I strapped on the Swiss seat, stood erect with my back to the gorge, leaned backwards & inched my way over the steep edge. When I reached the bottom alive and in one piece, I was so exhilarated that I raced up to do it again!

The people of Israel trusted God
and went right through the Red Sea
as though on dry ground.
Hebrews 11:29
(Living Bible)

Go;
be it done for you
as you have believed.
Matthew 8:13

Rise and go your way;
your faith has
made you well.
Luke 17:19

Fear not, stand firm,
and see the salvation
of the LORD.
Exodus 14:13

I give unto you power to tread on serpents
and scorpions, and over all the power of the
enemy; and nothing shall by any means hurt you.
Luke 10:19
(King James Version)

Blessed is the man who trusts in the LORD,
whose trust is the LORD.
He is like a tree planted by water,
that sends out its roots by the stream,
and does not fear when heat comes,
for its leaves remain green,
and is not anxious in the year of drought,
for it does not cease to bear fruit.
Jeremiah 17:7-8

Jesus asked them, "Do you believe I can
make you see?" "Yes, Lord," they told
him, "we do." Then he touched their eyes
and said, "Because of your faith it will
happen." And suddenly they could see!
Matthew 9:28-30
(Living Bible)

For as the body without the spirit is dead,
so faith without works is dead also.
James 2:26
(King James Version)

When he heard God's warning about the future,
Noah believed him even though there was then
no sign of a flood, and wasting no time, he
built the ark and saved his family.
Hebrews 11:7
(Living Bible)

And it was by faith that Joseph, as he neared
the end of his life, confidently spoke of God
bringing the people of Israel out of Egypt;
and he was so sure of it that he made them
promise to carry his bones with them when they
left!
Hebrews 11:22
(Living Bible)

It was faith that brought the walls of Jericho
tumbling down after the people of Israel had
walked around them seven days, as God had
commanded them.
Hebrews 11:30
(Living Bible)

For the Kingdom of God belongs to men who
have hearts as trusting as these little
children's.
Luke 18:16
(Living Bible)

With men this is impossible, but with God
all things are possible.
Matthew 19:26

It is your Father's good pleasure
to give you the kingdom.
Luke 12:32

If you have faith as a mustard seed,
you will say to this mountain, "Move from here
to there," and it will move; and nothing will
be impossible to you.
Matthew 17:20

FAITH DRAWS MY GOOD FROM THE INVISIBLE
INTO THE VISIBLE.

EVERYTHING I CONCEIVE AND NOW BELIEVE, I
WILL ACHIEVE!

I SAY YES TO MY GOOD!

I EXPECT MY GOOD TO COME AND I AM READY
TO RECEIVE IT!

I KNOW THAT A POWER GREATER THAN MYSELF
- THE SUPREME BEING - GOD -
IS RESPONDING TO ME IN A PERSONAL WAY.

I RECEIVE THE BEST BECAUSE I EXPECT THE
BEST.

THE GOOD THAT I SEEK IS EVEN NOW SEEKING
ME!

STRENGTH

I am at ease and at peace.

STRENGTH IS...

Strength is my capacity for sustained conviction and joy. No adversity can destroy my optimism & turn me back from my spiritual quest. Centered and poised in the presence of God, I move through the activities of this day easily and gracefully. I have a sparkle in my eye, a smile on my face, and a song in my heart.

The spirit of God within me is greater than any circumstance. God provides me with all the strength I need. God is with me in both the valley and on the mountain. I am part of the solution. I am calm and filled with peace. I relax and rest in the presence of God and I am refreshed. I know that God is working in and through my life and affairs. I rely on the spirit of God within me, an infinite resource of courage and strength.

I give life the light touch. I enjoy the people around me. I keep a smile on my face and a song in my heart, and I find God's goodness everywhere. I am a cheerful person. In every situation, I let feelings of fun, excitement, and adventure govern my outlook. My life and world are filled with harmony. I am a radiating center of the peace of God.

SYMBOLS OF STRENGTH

Old Testament - Samson

Samson in Hebrew means sunlike and sunny. He was noted for his great strength and for his victories over the Philistines. The Philistines, Goliath in particular, represent our greatest fears which we can overcome through our power of spiritual strength.

New Testament - Andrew

In Greek, Andrew means strong. Peter was introduced to Jesus by his brother Andrew. In times of crisis, Andrew looked beyond the problem to the solution. At the feeding of the five thousand it was Andrew who introduced a little boy with his picnic meal of five barley loaves and two small fishes to Jesus.

Color - Spring Green
Stone - Sapphire

FACE THE SUNSHINE
AND THE SHADOWS
WILL FALL BEHIND YOU.

****

They that wait upon the Lord
shall renew their strength.
They shall mount up with
wings like eagles;
they shall run
and not be weary;
they shall walk
and not faint.
Isaiah 40:31
(Living Bible)

Be of good cheer.
John 16:33

For you shall go out in joy,
and be led forth in peace;
the mountains and the hills before you
shall break forth into singing,
and all the trees of the field shall
clap their hands.
Isaiah 55:12

And your strength shall be renewed
day by day like morning dew.
Psalms 110:3
(Living Bible)

A glad heart makes a cheerful countenance...
A cheerful heart has a continual feast.
Proverbs 15:13,15

This is the day which the Lord has made;
let us rejoice and be glad in it.
Psalms 118:24

Be bold and strong!
Joshua 1:9
(Living Bible)

INNER PEACE

My second year in college, I bought my first car - a ten year old Volkswagen Beetle. Despite the spartan qualities, having wheels of my own was a great luxury. It even had AM radio! I waxed it often and loved my "Bug."

My wife, Janice, and I were recently married, but attending school 600 miles from each other. On Christmas break we shared an apartment in Toledo for two wonderful weeks. One day Jan returned tearfully to announce that the "Bug" had died in traffic - blown a rod. Now came the big decision - invest $600 in a new engine or buy another used Beetle for $1200. Being attached to "this" car, we replaced the engine.

Two days later Janice again appeared tearfully at the door of our apartment. This time her face and clothes were smudged with black. She had given my sister a ride in the back seat and the springs of the seat connected the posts of the car battery underneath. This started a fire in the back seat just as they pulled in front of their school.

After the fire trucks extinguished the fire, the interior had shriveled into black melted plastic. The sunvisor looked like a naked coat hanger. One of the firemen offered Janice $100 to take the car off her hands. After class, Janice bravely climbed into the wet and charred remains to drive back to our apartment.

As the tale unfolded, it was all I could do to suppress the laughter welling up inside. I was delighted Janice was ok - she was my real treasure, not the "Bug." Anger didn't cross my mind and certainly wouldn't have helped Janice or the situation. I reassured Janice that I still loved her and things would be fine...and they were! For another $300 we had the car reupholstered and it looked better and ran better than ever.

He determined that there should be a choir
leading the march,
clothed in sanctified garments
and singing the song
"His Lovingkindness Is Forever"
as they walked along
praising and thanking the Lord!
2 Chronicles 20:21
(Living Bible)

I will strengthen you;
I will help you;
I will uphold you
with my victorious right hand.
Isaiah 41:10
(Living Bible)

The LORD is my shepherd,
I shall not want;
he makes me lie down in green pastures.
He leads me beside still waters;
he restores my soul.
He leads me in paths of righteousness
for his name's sake.
Even though I walk through the valley of
the shadow of death, I fear no evil;
for thou art with me;
thy rod and thy staff,
they comfort me.
Thou preparest a table before me
in the presence of my enemies;
thou anointest my head with oil,
my cup overflows.
Surely goodness and mercy shall follow me
all the days of my life; and I
shall dwell in the house of the LORD forever.
Psalms 23

Be strong,
and let your heart
take courage.
Psalms 27:14

The battle is not yours
but God's...
You will
not need to fight in this battle;
take your position,
stand still,
and see
the victory of the LORD
on your behalf.
2 Chronicles 20:15,17

I love thee, O LORD,
my strength.

The LORD is my rock,
and my fortress,
and my deliverer.
Psalms 18:1-2

Blessed are those who dwell in thy house
...They go from strength to strength.
Psalms 84:4,7

Thou dost keep him in perfect peace,
whose mind is stayed on thee,
because he trusts in thee.
Isaiah 26:3

A tranquil mind
gives life to the flesh.
Proverbs 14:30

In returning and rest
you shall be saved;

in quietness and in trust
shall be your strength.
Isaiah 30:15

Be still,
and know
that I am God.
Psalms 46:10

The God of peace
will be with you.
Philippians 4:9

The LORD bless you and keep you:
The LORD make his face to shine upon you,
and be gracious to you:

The LORD lift up his countenance upon you,
and give you peace.
Numbers 6:24-26

THE SLEEPING GIANT WITHIN ME AWAKENS!

I RADIATE SELF - CONFIDENCE!

I AM AT MY BEST WHEN FACING A CHALLENGE BECAUSE I KEEP A LIGHT HEART AND A LIGHT TOUCH!

MY DAY IS FILLED WITH HAPPINESS AND FUN!

MY SONG IS BEAUTIFUL AND I SING IT.

IN THE SILENCE OF MY BEING I SHOUT WITH JOY!

MY HAPPY FACE IS A REFLECTION OF MY HAPPY HEART!

WISDOM AND GOOD JUDGMENT

**God's light shines through me and illumines
a clear path to my good.**

MY SIXTH SENSE

Wisdom and Good Judgment is my God given intuitive ability to clearly know the truth and to be divinely guided and directed at all times. God is my partner and counselor. The wisdom of God lights my way. God, the Way-Shower, knows and reveals the right answer and the right choice for every circumstance. As I follow God's instructions and guidance, my way is clear.

I respond with wisdom and good judgment in all situations that call for my decisions. I consider the needs and desires of others as well as those of my own. I create harmony with others. God's light shines on my path, and I progress in right and perfect ways.

I am wise with a wisdom greater than my own. I see clearly with a mind that is more illuminated than my own. With confidence, I now draw upon a higher wisdom that guides me in right choices and moves me to right action.

SYMBOLS OF WISDOM

Old Testament - Solomon

Solomon chose wisdom above riches and honor. Then all other things were added. Solomon was given a rare gift of intuition and did not rest his investigations on visible facts, but sought out inner motives. When two women claimed the same baby, he ordered the child divided in half and knew at once the real mother as the one who would give up the child to save it.

New Testament - James, son of Zebedee

James received personalized corrective guidance twice from Jesus. The first was when he and his brother John desired to bring down fire from heaven on an inhospitable Samaritan village and the second when they sought special positions of honor in heaven.

Color - Yellow
Stone - Agate

IF AT FIRST
YOU DON'T SUCCEED,

READ THE INSTRUCTIONS.

****

If you abide in My Word
- hold fast to my teachings
and live in accordance with them
- you are truly My disciples.

And you will know the truth,
and the truth will set you free.
John 8:32
(Amplified Bible)

Every one then who hears these words of mine
and does them will be like a wise man who
built his house upon rock; and the rain fell,
and the floods came, and the winds blew and
beat upon that house, but it did not fall,
because it had been founded on the rock.

And every one who hears these words of mine
and does not do them will be like the foolish
man who built his house upon sand; and the
rain fell, and the floods came, and the winds
blew and beat against that house, and it fell;
and great was the fall of it.
Matthew 7:24-27

Happy is the man who finds wisdom,
and the man who gets understanding,
for the gain from it is better than gain
from silver and its profit better than gold.

She is more precious than jewels,
and nothing you can desire can compare with
her. Long life is in her right hand;
in her left hand are riches and honor.

Her ways are ways of pleasantness,
and all her paths are peace. She
is a tree of life to those who lay hold of her;
those who hold her fast are called happy.
Proverbs 3:13-18

He opens their ears ... and gives them
wisdom and instruction.
Job 33:16
(Living Bible)

Speak, LORD, for thy servant hears.
1 Samuel 3:9

INTUITION

Janice and I met in June on summer break at the swimming pool back on the chicken farm. Sister, Lucy, had brought home her nursing school classmate for the weekend. After a summer romance, we resumed our respective college educations 600 miles apart. Thanksgiving weekend we chose to get married and did not see each other until the following summer, except for Christmas break.

Was this a wise thing for us to do? For us the answer is yes! We have been happily married twenty-one years and our wedding seems like yesterday. How did we know this was right for us? The answer is we trusted our feelings and followed our hearts. The wisdom of the heart is our sixth sense or intuition. The other reason for our success is that we accept and love each other unconditionally, without trying to change each other.

"Both dreams mean the same thing,"
Joseph told Pharaoh.
"God was telling you
what he is going to do here
in the land of Egypt.
The seven fat cows (and also
the seven fat, well formed heads of grain)
mean that there are seven years
of prosperity ahead.
The seven skinny cows (and also
the seven thin and withered heads of grain)
indicate that there will be seven years of famine
following the seven years of prosperity.
... Gather into the royal storehouses
all the excess crops of the next seven years,
so that there will be enough to eat
when the seven years of famine come."
... Pharaoh said to him,
"Since God has revealed the meaning
of the dreams to you,
you are the wisest man in the country!
I am hereby appointing you
to be in charge of this entire project.
What you say goes,
throughout the land of Egypt,
I alone will outrank you."
Genesis 41:25-40
(Living Bible)

What no eye has seen,
nor ear heard,
nor heart of man conceived,
what God has prepared
for those who love him,
God has revealed to us
through the Spirit.
1 Corinthians 2:9-10

My angel goes before you.
Exodus 23:23

The LORD went before them
by day
in a pillar of cloud
to lead them along the way,
and by night
in a pillar of fire
to give them light.
Exodus 13:21

In paths that they have not known
I will guide them.
Isaiah 42:16

Call to me
and I will answer you,
and will tell you
great and hidden things
which you have not known.
Jeremiah 33:3

A mirror reflects a man's face,
but what he is really like
is shown
by the kind of friends
he chooses.
Proverbs 27:19
(Living Bible)

Teach me thy way,
O LORD;
and lead me
on a level path.
Psalms 27:11

The Lord ... was glad that Solomon
had asked for wisdom.

So he replied, "... I will give you
a wiser mind than anyone else
has ever had or ever will have!

And I will also give you
what you didn't ask for -
riches and honor!
1 Kings 3:10-13
(Living Bible)

He who walks with wise men
becomes wise.
Proverbs 13:20

Many counselors bring success.
Proverbs 15:22

The advice of a wise man
refreshes like water
from a mountain spring.

Those accepting it
become aware of the pitfalls on ahead.
Proverbs 13:14
(Living Bible)

Do not judge by appearances,
but judge with right judgment.
John 7:24

I LISTEN TO THE VOICE WITHIN ME.

I FOLLOW MY HUNCHES AND INSTINCTS.

RESULTS ARE MY GURU!

I FOCUS ON PLEASING RESULTS.

GOD'S INFINITE INTELLIGENCE INSPIRES,
INFORMS, DIRECTS AND GUIDES ME.

I MAKE WISE CHOICES AND GREAT DECISIONS!

EVERYTHING IN MY LIFE IS VIEWED IN A NEW
LIGHT, SO I FOLLOW NEW PATHS TO HIGH
PLACES!

LOVE

My life is overflowing with happy, harmonizing, love-filled relationships.

THE GREATEST GIFT

Love is the spirit of God in me loving all creation. Through me, love is born again. Through love I live with God again. I live and move in the glow of God's pure love. My relationships are peaceful and harmonious. I radiate love to all people and express sincere appreciation to them for making my life more rich and meaningful.

God's love fills me, and I do my work joyfully. Love lends creativity to all my endeavors. Love brings order and harmony to all my efforts. Love assures success and opens the way for positive changes. My work is transformed into a work of love and joy. My work blesses others and honors God, and I find happiness and satisfaction in doing it.

I am God's beloved child, with whom He is well pleased. The more love I express, the more love I have to give. Love is the bounty of God's inexhaustible storehouse, and I am an expression of God's love in my world.

SYMBOLS OF LOVE

Old Testament - David

David loved beauty, poetry, and music. He charmed Saul with his songs and harp music & danced before the Ark of the Covenant when moving it to Jerusalem. He was Israel's favorite king and prophets pointed to a future David who would restore Israel's fortunes. The Gospels refer to Jesus twelve times as "Son of David."

New Testament - John

John is described as the disciple whom Jesus loved. After the Last Supper, Jesus washed the disciples' feet and revealed one of them would betray him. Peter signed to John who leaned back on Jesus's breast and said, "Lord who is it?" From the cross Jesus entrusted the care of his mother Mary to John.

Color - Pink
Stone - Emerald

CHARM IS THE ABILITY
TO MAKE SOMEONE ELSE THINK

THAT BOTH OF YOU
ARE PRETTY WONDERFUL.

****

Love one another;

for love is of God;
and every one that loveth
is born of God,
and knoweth God.

He that loveth not
knoweth not God;

for God is love.
1 John 4:7-8
(King James Version)

Put on love,
which binds everything together
in perfect harmony.
Colossians 3:14

The father said to his servants, "Bring quickly
the best robe, and put it on him; and put a
ring on his hand, and shoes on his feet; and
bring the fatted calf and kill it, and let us
make merry; for this my son was dead, and is
found." And they began to make merry.
Luke 15:22-24

You are precious in my eyes,
and honored,
and I love you.
Isaiah 43:4

He brought me to the banqueting house,
and his banner over me was love.
Song of Solomon 2:4

God loves us,

and we feel this warm love
everywhere within us
because God
has given us
the Holy Spirit.
Romans 5:5
(Living Bible)

THE JOY OF LOVE

When I was four years old, I looked more like a girl than a boy. My hair had never been cut and I had long blond golden locks. I was the first born and mom and I would often do our nails together with bright shiny clear nail polish.

One day I had my first bubble bath. Giant mountains of white fluffy bubbles floated all around me and I swatted them into the air with glee. I was small then and could lay down full length in the tub. Mom was humming and shampooing my long "goldilocks" when she suddenly got a notion.

She tastefully spiralled my hair up on top of my head into a huge curly top and proceeded to laugh uncontrollably. I had no idea what was funny but laughed and laughed too because of her merriment. Then mom showed me my hair in a hand mirror and resumed laughing hysterically. I laughed with her and felt a warm glow of being loved all over my body.

Make love your aim.
1 Corinthians 14:1

If I speak in the tongues of men and of angels,
but have not love, I am a noisy gong or a
clanging cymbal. And if I have prophetic
powers, and understand all mysteries and all
knowledge, and if I have all faith, so as to
remove mountains, but have not love, I am
nothing. If I give away all I have, and if
I deliver my body to be burned, but have not
love, I gain nothing.

Love is patient and kind; love is not jealous
or boastful; it is not arrogant or rude. Love
does not insist on its own way; it is not
irritable or resentful; it does not rejoice at
wrong, but rejoices in the right. Love bears
all things, believes all things, hopes all things,
endures all things.
1 Corinthians 13:1-7

My prayer for you
is that you will overflow
more and more
with love for others.
Philippians 1:9
(Living Bible)

Be beautiful inside,

in your hearts,
with the lasting charm.
1 Peter 3:4
(Living Bible)

```
  *   *   *       *   *   *
    *           *           *
    *                         *
  *         They are rich       *
  *                             *
  *             who             *
    *                         *
    *       have friends.     *
      *                     *
        *                 *
          *             *
            *         *
                *
```

Walk in love

- esteeming and delighting
in one another.
Ephesians 5:2
(Amplified Bible)

Faith, hope, love abide,
these three;
but the greatest of these
is love.
1 Corinthians 13:15

Love your neighbor
as yourself.
Galatians 5:14

A Samaritan... had compassion,
and went to him
and bound up his wounds,
pouring on oil and wine;
then set him on his own beast
and brought him to an inn,
and took care of him...

Go and do likewise.
Luke 10:33-37

God's love has been poured
into our hearts
through the Holy Spirit.
Romans 5:5

Let love
guide your life.
Colossians 3:14
(Living Bible)

Love each other
just as much
as I love you.

Your strong love
for each other

will prove to the world
that you are
My disciples.
John 13:34-35
(Living Bible)

God is love,

and he who abides in love
abides in God,
and God abides in him.
1 John 4:16

Love the Lord your God

with all your heart,
and with all your soul,
and with all your mind.
Matthew 22:37

Show hospitality to strangers,
for thereby
some have entertained angels unawares.
Hebrews 13:2

THE WARM LIGHT OF GOD'S LOVE FLOODS MY BEING!

I LIKE PEOPLE AND PEOPLE LIKE ME!

I RADIATE LOVE AND I ATTRACT LOVE.

MY CUP OF GOOD IS RUNNING OVER!

MY HEART SINGS A SONG OF PRAISE AND GRATITUDE.

GREAT IS MY GIFT TO THE WORLD, FOR I GIVE MYSELF AT MY BEST!

I LET THE GOODNESS OF ME BURST FORTH AS A BLESSING UPON ALL THE WORLD!

POWER OF THE SPOKEN WORD

**The power of God enables me
to leap over walls of limitation.**

OUT THE ABUNDANCE OF THE HEART, THE MOUTH SPEAKS

The Power of the Spoken Word is the creative power that converts my spoken or silent thoughts and feelings into living fact. My personal word is recreated as my personal world. What I decree, becomes established for me.

I am building a spiritual conscious- ness. My thoughts are the building blocks of my consciousess which in turn determines the quality of my life. My consciousness - all that I am aware of in spirit, soul, and body - is the founda- tion upon which I build my life.

I choose to think thoughts that encourage and sustain me. Because my thoughts affect the way I act and the way I respond to others, I take time to evaluate the kind of thoughts I think. When I make a new, better choice of thoughts, I change my attitudes, habits, and overall behavior for better.

God's spirit is at the center of my being. From this perfect center, I form new thoughts and outlooks. I think thoughts of health, knowing that God is the source of my wellness. I think thoughts of prosperity, recognizing that God's abundance prospers me. I continually update the quality of my thinking.

If I am watching a television program that I do not find informative or enjoyable, I can either change the channel or turn off the set. I have the same right and privilege of selection in the kind of thoughts I think and the emotions I express. My thoughts and feelings have creative power for me to use in establishing and maintaining a happy and successful life.

I think on divine inspired thoughts before I speak and act. When I allow my thoughts to be transformed by God before I speak, I give myself the opportunity to use words that uplift, encourage, and heal. I speak positive, loving words that are affirmations of truth.

In my home and work I use words of encouragement, praise, and appreciation. I speak to others in the way I want them to speak to me, and initiate a circle of productive communication. I speak words that convey my positive feelings and lead to greater understanding between myself and others. My loving attitude spreads like ripples on the water, reaching out to family, friends, and co-workers. I dedicate my spoken words to the glory of God and the empowerment of all who hear me.

SYMBOLS OF POWER OF THE SPOKEN WORD

Old Testament - Elijah

In a contest with the priests of Baal on Mount Carmel, the priests leaped around their altar all day with no answer. Then Elijah prayed and God rained fire from heaven consuming the sacrifice. When Elijah predicted the end of the three year drought, a great storm arose. Elijah exited to heaven in a blazing chariot. Jesus consulted with Elijah and Moses at his transfiguration on the mountain.

New Testatment - Phillip

Phillip ran to tell his brother he had met the predicted Messiah. When Nathanael was skeptical, Phillip replied, "Come and see." At the Last Supper Phillip asked Jesus to show them the Father. Jesus responded, "He who has seen me has seen the Father."

Color - Purple
Stone - Onyx

SINGING AT THE LAST SUPPER

Praise of God is one of Scripture's major themes. Praise comes from a Latin word meaning "value" or "price." Thus, to give praise to God is to proclaim His merit or worth. Many terms are used to express this in the Bible, including "glory," "blessing," "thanksgiving," and "hallelujah," the last being a translation of the Hebrew for "Praise the Lord."

The Hebrew title of the book of Psalms ("Praises") comes from the same root as "hallelujah" and Psalms 113-118 have been specially designated the "Hallel" ("praise") psalms.

After the Last Supper Jesus and the disciples sang a hymn before going to the Mount of Olives (Mark 14:26). The hymn they sang was likely the Hallel, a song of praise sung each year by Hebrews in their homes to celebrate the Passover.

WHEN YOU SPEAK,

BE SURE THE THINGS YOU SAY
ARE AN IMPROVEMENT
OVER SILENCE.

****

Heaven and earth will disappear,
but My words remain forever.
Matthew 24:35
(Living Bible)

For as the rain and the snow come down
from heaven, and return not thither but
water the earth, making it bring forth
and sprout, giving seed to the sower and
bread to the eater, so shall my word be
that goes forth from my mouth; it shall
not return to me empty, but it shall
accomplish that which I purpose, and
prosper in the thing for which I sent it.
Isaiah 55:10-11

Just speak a word from where You are, and my
servant boy will be healed!
I know, because I am under authority of my
superior officers, and I have authority over
my men.   I only need to say "Go!" and they go;
or "Come!" and they come;   and to my slave,
"Do this or that," and he does it.   So just
say, "Be healed!" and my servant will be well
again!
Luke 7:7-8
(Living Bible)

The Holy Spirit's power was in my words,
proving to those who heard them
that the message was from God.
1 Corinthians 2:4
(Living Bible)

And they were amazed at His teaching,
for His word was with authority
and ability and weight
and power.
Luke 4:32
(Amplified Bible)

The dead shall hear My voice -
the voice of the Son of God -
and those who listen
shall live.
John 5:25
(Living Bible)

A NEW VOCABULARY

In a class called Alpha Truth Awareness by itinerate motivational speaker, Vrle Minto, I learned the concept that the words I think and speak have power to shape my life. I had an old pattern of releasing long sentences of emotional explicatives when faced with sudden unexpected adversities. I honed them to a fine art on the chicken farm as a boy when I would bark a shin on a chicken troth or impale my head on an overhead beam.

Now I was informed that my life experience would be improved if I consciously removed negative words from my vocabulary and replaced them with positive ones. If I caught myself in the act of an old habit pattern, I was to say "Clear, clear" and then "Love, love, love." This worked great for me. Gradually the sentences became shorter and ultimately disappeared. I felt better about myself and I no longer polluted the air waves of people around me.

Besides swear words I also cancelled out many words with negative connota-

tions. Instead of using the word "sorry",
I would ask "How can I help?" Instead of
making the quality of my days dependent
on the weather, I chose to enjoy everyday
and make my own sunshine. Life became
fun and I felt like a little child again.
     My favorite assignment was affirma-
tions. Each morning, I would sing them
in the shower "I AM GREAT, I AM GREAT,
I AM GREAT-I AM RICH, I AM RICH, I AM
RICH." I would also sing them in the
second and third person "CODY YOU ARE
GREAT" & "CODY IS GREAT." After a few
weeks I genuinely would wake up feeling
great. As my self-esteem grew, so did my
business. Within one year my veterinary
hospital which had plateaued previously,
miraculously doubled its services!

YOUR AFFIRMATION ASSIGNMENT:

_____   Select three affirmations from
          this book and print them in large
          letters on 3 x 5 cards and place
          them on your bathroom mirrior.

_____   Repeat them enthusiastically three
          times each morning and evening for
          three weeks.

_____   Expect miraclulous results.

He cried with a loud voice,
"Lazarus, come out."

The dead man came out,
his hands and feet
bound with bandages,
and his face wrapped with a cloth.
Jesus said to them,
"Unbind him,
and let him go."
John 11:43-44

The words
that I have spoken to you
are spirit and life.
John 6:63

As He was praying,
His face began to shine,
and His clothes became dazzling white
and blazed with light.
Luke 9:29
(Living Bible)

You **LAUGH**
when something amusing
enters your mind,

you **CRY**
when something sad
enters your mind,

you **GROW PALE**
with anger or fear,
you **BLUSH**
with embarrassment.

It is always **A THOUGHT**
which brings different
reactions to the body.

The body is simply
an instrument
which the **MIND**
uses to express its emotions.

A word fitly spoken
is like apples of gold
in a setting of silver.
Proverbs 25:11

Let the words of my mouth
and the meditation of my heart
be acceptable in thy sight,
O LORD.
Psalms 19:14

The mind of the wise
makes his speech judicious,
and adds persuasiveness
to his lips.

Pleasant words are like a honeycomb,
sweetness to the soul
and health to the body.
Proverbs 16:23-24

Whatever is true, whatever is honorable,
whatever is just, whatever is pure,
whatever is lovely, whatever is gracious,

if there is any excellence,
if there is anything worthy of praise,
think about these things.
Philippians 4:8

Good news
refreshes the bones.
Proverbs 15:30

Whatever you ask in prayer,
believe that you have received it,
and it will be yours.
Mark 11:24

The crew decided to draw straws to see which
of them had offended the gods and caused
this terrible storm; and Jonah
drew the short one...

Then they picked up Jonah and threw him
overboard into the raging sea -
and the storm stopped!

...The Lord had arranged for a great fish
to swallow Jonah. And Jonah was inside
the fish three days and three nights.

Then Jonah prayed to the Lord his God
from inside the fish...
And the Lord ordered the fish to spit up
Jonah on the beach,
and it did.
Jonah 1:7-2:10
(Living Bible)

Ask,
and it will be given you;
seek and you will find;
knock,
and it will be opened to you.
For every one who asks receives,
and he who seeks finds,
and to him who knocks
it will be opened.
Matthew 7:7-8

I SPEAK ONLY POSITIVE UPLIFTING POWERFUL
WORDS TO MYSELF AND OTHERS.

MY PRAYERS SEND POWERFUL SURGES OF
SPIRTUAL ENERGY TO EACH OF MY FRIENDS.

MY AFFIRMATIONS ARE THE TRUTH OF MY INNER
BEING.

THEY INSPIRE AND MOTIVATE ME AND BRING
ABOUT AMAZING CHANGES IN MY LIFE.

GOD RESPONDS IMMEDIATELY TO MY PRAYERS,
FULFILLING MY EVERY REQUEST.

MY PRAYERS ARE ANSWERED IMMEDIATELY AND
DRAMATICALLY!

I DELIGHT IN THE AMAZING RESULTS MY
PRAYERS FOR CHANGE ARE BRINGING!

CREATIVE IMAGINATION

My life has infinite possibilities.

BLUEPRINT FOR SUCCESS

Creative Imagination is the spiritual power of visualization that gives form to all things. I conceive only positive mental images knowing that my life becomes what I picture it to be. My external life is but a reflection of the secret images I carry in my mind. My imagination is a creative power and I use it wisely. Imagination can take me in many directions. I choose to let it take me to my highest good. All the wonderful discoveries that have ever been made, were first ideas conceived in the imagination. There are no limits to the heights that God's creative imagination can take me.

God's ideas come to me through many channels: the Bible, books, conversations, thoughts, and prayers. I use my creative imagination to mold divine ideas. God gives me ideas freely, and I put them to creative use. I envision the best for me and my loved ones. When I hold to that vision, I formulate a life that is positive, enriching, and satisfying. My dreams and visions are the blueprints for my future successes.

SYMBOLS OF CREATIVE IMAGINATION

Old Testament - Joseph

Joseph wore a coat of many colors and saw his family bow down to him in a dream. After being sold into slavery, he predicted the future from Pharoh's dream, became govenor of Egypt, and saved his family from famine. He foresaw the Exodus and made his people promise to take his bones with them when they left.

New Testament - Nathanael (Bartholemew)

Jesus commended Nathanael for his candor and frankness (lack of guile). Nathanael saw in Jesus "the Son of God" at their first encounter. Jesus told Nathanael, "You shall see greater things than these...you will see heaven opened, and the angels of God ascending and descending upon the Son of man."

Color - Light Blue
Stone - Carnelian

THE POOREST MAN
IS NOT HE WHO
IS WITHOUT A CENT,

BUT HE WHO
IS WITHOUT A DREAM.

****

God speaks again and again, in dreams,
in visions of the night when deep sleep
falls on men as they lie on their beds.
Job 33:14
(Living Bible)

Jacob ... stopped to camp at sundown,
he found a rock for a headrest
and lay down to sleep,
and dreamed that a staircase
reached from earth to heaven,
and he saw the angels of God
going up and down upon it.
At the top of the stairs stood the Lord.
...He said, "...The ground you are lying on
is yours! I will give it to you
and to your descendants.
For you will have descendants
as many as the dust!

... I am with you,
and will protect you
wherever you go."
... Jacob woke up.
"God lives here!"
he exclaimed...
"This is the awesome entrance to Heaven!"
Genesis 28:10-17
(Living Bible)

The LORD appeared to Solomon
in a dream by night;
and God said,
"Ask what I shall give you."
1 Kings 3:5

The following February...
another message from the Lord
came to Zechariah...
in a vision in the night...
THE ANGEL showed me (in my vision)
Joshua the High Priest
standing before the Angel of the Lord...
Joshua's clothing was filthy...
The Angel said, "Remove his filthy clothing...
I have taken away your sins,
and now I am giving you
these fine new clothes...
You are illustrations of the good things
to come... you will live in peace
and prosperity.
Zechariah 1:7-3:10
(Living Bible)

THINK CREATIVELY

A little Creative Imagination goes a long way for the aspiring entrepreneur. When my dad got out of college, he set out to revolutionize the egg industry by offering eggs guaranteed less than ten days old (grade AA) compared to the old standard of less than 30 days old (grade A).

Starting from scratch dad bought a farm, cut logs in the woods, took them to a saw mill, and had an old fashioned barn raising. He raised day old chicks to become hens, processed the eggs and was off to the "big city" (Toledo).

Housewives were startled to hear "cluck, cluck, cluck" as they arrived in the egg section of the supermarkets. The sign over her cage proclaimed "Clara, Queen of Hen Motel". The egg cartons proclaimed "Fresh eggs, hot from the hen!" Today's egg would be in the cage as Clara clucked proudly into her vanity mirror and pecked busily at her well earned grain.

Dad's business blossomed and he quickly became a major egg wholesaler for Toledo offering "quality eggs for our fine customers".

IMAGINEERING

Walt Disney's wonderful characters and stories come from his **Imagineering Department.** You can become the architect of your spectacular life by creating your own creativity department. Cut out words and pictures from magazines that portray your goals and place them on walls, mirrors, poster boards, and in photo albums. Look at the pictures often and visualize the joy of the experiences in detail. Include all areas of your life - physical, mental, spiritual growth, career, prosperity, relationships, travel, and self esteem. As Flip Wilson says, "What you see is what you get!"

CHECK OFF YOUR IMAGINEERING ASSIGNMENTS AS THEY ARE COMPLETED

____ **Image wall**
____ **Image mirror**
____ **Image poster**
____ **Image photo album**

I the LORD
make myself known to him
in a vision,

I speak with him
in a dream.
Numbers 12:6

And being warned of God in a dream that
they should not return to Herod, they departed
into their own country another way.

And when they were departed, behold, the
angel of the Lord appeareth to Joseph in a
dream, saying, Arise, and take the young child
and his mother, and flee into Egypt.
Matthew 2:12-13
(King James Version)

The Lord said to Paul
one night in a vision,
"Do not be afraid,
but speak
and do not be silent;
for I am with you.
Acts 18:9

Write the vision,

and make it plain.

Habakkuk 2:2

I HAVE A DREAM AND A VISION.

MY HEART'S DESIRES ARE:

1. _____

2. _____

3. _____

4. _____

I will pour out my spirit on all flesh;
your sons and daughters shall prophesy,
your old men shall dream dreams,
and your young men shall see visions.
Joel 2:28

One day as Moses was tending the flock...
the Angel of Jehovah appeared to him as
a flame of fire in a bush... the Lord
told him... "I am going to send you to
Pharaoh, to demand that he let you lead
my people out of Egypt."
Exodus 3:1-10
(Living Bible)

One day late in June,
when I was thirty years old,
the heavens were suddenly opened to me
and I saw visions from God.
...From his waist up,
he seemed to be all glowing bronze,
dazzling like fire;
and from his waist down
he seemed to be entirely flame,
and there was a glowing halo
like a rainbow all around him.
That was the way the glory of the Lord
appeared to me.
... And the Spirit entered into me
as he spoke ... "I am sending you
to give them my messages ...
And whether they listen or not,
(for remember, they are rebels),
they will at least know
they have had a prophet among them.
Ezekiel 1:1-2:5
(Living Bible)

GOD SPEAKS IN VISIONS

The Lord spoke to him in a vision,
calling, "Ananias...go over to...
Paul of Tarsus...

I have shown him a vision
of a man named Ananias
coming in and laying his hands on him
so that he can see again!"

"But Lord," exclaimed Ananias,
"I have heard about the terrible things
this man has done to
the believers in Jerusalem..."

But the Lord said,
"Go and do what I say.
For Paul is my chosen instrument
to take My message
to the nations and before Kings."
Acts 9:10-15
(Living Bible)

THE NEW JERUSALEM

And I, John,
saw the Holy City,
the new Jerusalem,
coming down from God
out of heaven.

It was a glorious sight,
beautiful as a bride
at her wedding.

I heard a loud shout from the throne
saying, "Look, the home of God
is now among men,

and He will live with them
and they will be His people."
Revelation 21:2-3
(Living Bible)

I AM THE ARCHITECT OF MY SPECTACULAR LIFE.

MY LIFE BECOMES WHAT I PICTURE IT TO BE.

I MAKE ONLY HAPPY PICTURES WITH MY MIND!

SEEING IS BELIEVING.

WHAT I SEE IS WHAT I GET!

I STRETCH MY MIND TO EXCITING NEW CONCEPTS AND MY WORLD EXPANDS ACCORDINGLY.

I GROW TO THE STATURE OF MY DREAMS.

SPIRITUAL UNDERSTANDING

I celebrate my uniqueness!

GOD IS MY PARTNER

Spiritual Understanding is my awakened awareness of my spiritual nature and heritage. God's presence is within me. God and I are one - therefore, all things are working together for my highest good.

Divine intelligence is active in me; I think clearly and learn easily. I am one with the mind of God. Tapping into a reservoir of divine intelligence, I gain new understanding, enlightment, and illumination. My potential is boundless.

I am both a student and a teacher. I am open and receptive to new ideas and experiences. Each day I learn and grow in knowlege of spiritual principles and laws of universal truths. I support and encourage others and help them on their upward journey.

God and I are partners. Together, we are triumphant. I am a hero on the field of life. The dictionary defines hero as: "A figure of divine descent endowed with great ability and admired for his acheivements and noble qualities." This definition is who I am.

I am God's own creation, a spiritual

being par excellence. I am endowed with
unlimited   potential.   I   develop and
express   my   spiritual   identity   to   a
greater degree each day. I celebrate my
true self and excerise spiritual mastery.
I open my mind to what already is, and
what already is, is wonderful. I am a
beloved   child   of God   and   the radiant
light of God   shines in me, through me,
and for me. Jesus said   the kingdom of
heaven   is like leaven in flour. Just as
leaven   lightens   and   increases   bread
dough,   God's teachings   raise my   consciousness and expand my mind.

SYMBOLS OF SPIRITUAL UNDERSTANDING

Old Testament - Daniel

Daniel was an Israeli youth of nobility, exiled to Babylon. He prayed three times daily facing Jerusalem, ate only vegetables and water, and was skilled in dream interpretation. When he was thrown into the lion's den, an angel shut the lion's mouths. At a banquet, he was the only one able to understand "the writing on the wall" and correctly predicted the fall of Babylon.

New Testament - Thomas

At the Last Supper, Jesus remarked "I go and prepare a place for you," and Thomas queried, "How can we know the way?" Jesus elucidated, "I am the way." Thomas sought physical evidence of Jesus' resurrection, but when convinced of the miracle exclaimed, "My Lord and my God!"

Color - Gold
Stone - Chrysolite

WE LEARN FROM EXPERIENCE.

PARENTS NEVER WAKE UP
THEIR SECOND BABY
JUST TO SEE IT SMILE.

****

The Counselor,
the Holy Spirit,
whom the Father will send
in my name,
he will teach you
all things.
John 14:26

A farmer was sowing grain in his fields...

As he scattered the seed across the ground,
some fell beside a path,
and the birds came and ate it...

But some fell on good soil,
and produced a crop
that was 30, 60 and even
100 times as much
as he had planted...

The hard path where some of the seed fell
represents the heart of a person
who hears the good news about the Kingdom
and doesn't understand it...

The good ground represents
the heart of a man
who listens to the message
and understands it.
Matthew 13:2-23
(Living Bible)

The measure of thought and study
you give to the truth you hear

will be the measure
of virtue and knowledge
that comes back to you.
Mark 4:24
(Amplified Bible)

Be careful therefore
how you listen
for to him
who has spiritual knowledge
will more be given.
Luke 8:18
(Amplified Bible)

STUDY GOD

Whatever you focus on expands. My senior year in high school I picked physics as my primary subject to master. I read ahead and completed all the homework questions at the end of the chapters. The physics teacher let me borrow the answer book so I could grade myself. Later he gave me other physics books to review that the school was considering purchasing.

At the Ohio State Scholastic Team Contest, I took the hardest physics test I had ever seen. When my teacher asked how it went, I was sure I had totally bombed out. What a surprise when a few weeks later it was announced over the school PA system that I had placed sixth in the state of Ohio! Pretty good for a farm kid in a small rural school on a self-directed home study course.

This book is a self-directed home study guide for spiritual understanding & growth for you. How much you benefit is proportional to the amount of time and study you put into it. Fifteen minutes each morning reading selected Scriptures from this book and practicing the affirmations will set the tone for God moments thru your upcoming day. The time is well spent since you are more efficient and productive when you are centered and happy.

Fifteen minutes at night with God's word is an excellent way to unwind and relax your mind before bedtime. You will sleep much more peacefully than if you watch the evening TV action/thriller and have much better dreams. You will also be studying God's word when your subconscious mind is most receptive to new programing-just before bed and just after waking.

STEPS I WILL TAKE TO UNDERSTAND GOD BETTER:

____   Scripture reading each morning

____   Scripture reading each evening

____   Answer the question - how does this reading apply to me today

The intelligent man
is always open
to new ideas.

In fact,
he looks for them.
Proverbs 18:15
(Living Bible)

No one puts new wine into old wineskins;

if he does,
the wine will burst the skins,
and the wine is lost,
and so are the skins;
but new wine is for fresh skins.
Mark 2:22

Teach a child
to choose the right path,

and when he is older
he will remain upon it.
Proverbs 22:6
(Living Bible)

He opens their ears to instruction ...
If they hearken and serve him,
they complete their days
in prosperity,
and their years
in pleasantness.
Job 36:10,11

Asked by the Pharisees when the kingdom of God
would come, He replied to them saying, The
kingdom of God does not come with signs to
be observed or visible display.

Nor will people say, Look!   Here it is!   or,
See it is there!   For behold, the kingdom of
of God is within you in your hearts and among
you surrounding you.
Luke 17:20-21
(Amplified Bible)

"What is the Kingdom like?"   He asked.
"How can I illustrate it?

It is like a tiny mustard seed planted
in a garden;   soon it grows into a tall
bush, and the birds live among its branches.
It is like yeast kneaded into dough,
which works unseen until it has risen
high and light."
Luke 13:18-21
(Living Bible)

The eternal God
is your dwelling place,
and underneath
are the everlasting arms.
Deuteronomy 33:27

You are God's temple,
... God's Spirit dwells in you.
1 Corinthians 3:16

Here there cannot be Greek and Jew,
circumcised and uncircumcised,
barbarian, Scythian,
slave, free man,
but Christ is all,
and in all.
Colossians 3:11

You are gods,
sons of the Most High,
all of you.
Psalms 82:6

We are children
of God.
Romans 8:16

Keep on growing

in spiritual knowledge
and insight.
Philippians 1:9
(Living Bible)

For now we see
in a mirror dimly,

but then face to face.
Now I know in part;
then I shall understand fully,

even as I have been
fully understood.
1 Corinthians 13:12

GOD IS ALL

both visible
and invisible.

One Presence,
ONE MIND,
One Power is all.

This One that is all
is Perfect Life
Perfect Love
and Perfect Substance.

**I am
an individualized expression
of God.**

I am ever one with
this Perfect Life,
Perfect Love,
and
Perfect
Substance.

(Unity Statement of Being)

I AM AN INDIVIDUALIZED EXPRESSION OF GOD.

I LET THE CHRIST IN ME SHINE FORTH!

I SEE MYSELF AS GOD SEES ME - HEALTHY, HAPPY, WHOLE AND FREE.

I UNDERSTAND AND PRACTICE UNIVERSAL SPIRITUAL PRINCIPLES.

I SEE ONLY SOLUTIONS AND ABUNDANCE!

EACH DEMONSTRATION IS PROOF THAT I AM LIVING IN A SPIRITUAL UNIVERSE.

I KNOW THAT LIFE IS GOOD AND GOD IS WATCHING OVER ME!

WILL

I live from fourth dimensional thinking.

GOD'S WILL IS GOODWILL

Will is my mind's decision making power that brings dynamic spiritual forces into play to acheive my inspired choices and exciting objectives.

God's will for me is always for my highest good. God's will for me is that I am healthy, prosperous, and at peace. Through God's spirit within me, I have the ability, authority, and freedom to make choices that lead to success and fulfillment.

Choosing the best is my goal. I establish positive new patterns in my life. Step-by-step, I accomplish the goals I desire in my life.

God is in charge of my life. I choose God's will for me, not my own. I make right choices when I choose to serve that which is for the highest and best for me and for all concerned.

As I outline my goals, I leave room in my plans and prayers for happy surprises. God's good can appear in seemingly improbable ways and through unexpected channels. My prayer is, "This, Lord, or something better."

SYMBOLS OF WILL

Old Testament - Joshua

Joshua was the Israeli commander during the move into the Promised Land. His brilliant planning and strategy brought military and political success. He was also a spiritual leader, harmonizing his people, communicating God's will, and leading in the covenant renewal.

New Testament - Matthew

Levi, the tax collector, transformed his life and became known as Matthew, "the gift of God." He answered Jesus' call, "Follow me" and hosted a great feast at his home with Jesus the guest of honor. Trained in accounting, he carefully recorded the teachings of Jesus about the principles upon which life is to be lived under the rule of God.

Color - Silver
Stone - Beryl

**GREAT MINDS
HAVE PURPOSES,**

**OTHERS
HAVE WISHES.**

****

Do not be conformed to this world
but be transformed
by the renewal of your mind,

that you may prove
what is the will of God,
what is good
and acceptable
and perfect.
Romans 12:2

Follow me.

For what shall it profit a man
if he shall gain the whole world,
and lose
his own soul?
Mark 8:34,36
(King James Version)

Happy are those who
are strong in the Lord,
who want above all else
to follow your steps.

When they walk
through the Valley of Weeping
it will become
a place of springs

where pools of blessing
and refreshment
collect after rains!
Psalms 84:5-6
(Living Bible)

Where you go
I will go,

and where you lodge
I will lodge.
Ruth 1:16

THE CHAIRMAN OF THE BOARD

Will is the chairman of the board, the chief executive officer of our mind. The decisions we make through our power of Will literally chart our course as we move through our lives.

In fifth grade, a strange man appeared in my classroom tooting a tuba, trombone, clarinet, and a flute. Shortly thereafter, I found myself taking trombone lessons. One night, practicing out in the egghouse, I looked myself directly in a little mirror and vowed, "I will master the trombone!"

That commitment set in motion a whole new world of wonderful and exciting experiences for me during the next eight years. In marching band we went to parades all over the county in the summer and to all the football games in the fall. Once we got new uniforms and my hat was too small. As we high stepped past the grandstand bobbing our heads up and down my hat flew off behind me. As I grabbed for the hat, I released the slide and it flew forward ahead. At that moment we pivoted and halted before the stands. As I played an imaginary slide

on my trombone during the serious alma
mater laughter emanated from the stands.
Other memorable events were solos at
competitions, symphonic band, state FFA
band, and college ROTC band.

We take charge of our lives by
setting specific goals. Each new decision we make today creates a new reality
in our lives tomorrow. Choose wisely and
aim high!

VICTORY LIST

List major successes from your life that
resulted from your goals and decisions.

1. _____

2. _____

3. _____

4. _____

5. _____

6. _____

7. _____

8. _____

9. _____

For a day in thy courts is better
than a thousand elsewhere.

I would rather be a doorkeeper
in the house of my God
than dwell in the tents
of wickedness.

For the LORD God
is a sun and shield;

he bestows favor and honor.

No good thing does the LORD withhold
from those who walk uprightly.
Psalms 84:10-11

You will decide on a matter,
and it will be
established for you,
and light
will shine on your ways.
Job 22:28

We know that in everything
God works for good
with those who love him,
who are called
according to his purpose.
Romans 8:28

Many are the plans
in the mind of a man,

but it is the purpose of the LORD
that will be established.
Proverbs 19:21

A man's mind
plans his way,

but the LORD
directs his steps.
Proverbs 16:9

The Lord gave them a desire
to rebuild his Temple;

so they all gathered
in early September...
and volunteered their help.
Haggai 1:14-15
(Living Bible)

Not my will,
but thine,
be done.
Luke 22:42
(King James Version)

I seek not my own will
but the will
of him who sent me.
John 5:30 RSV

While he was still speaking to the people,
behold, his mother and his brothers stood
outside, asking to speak to him.
But he replied to the man who told him,
"Who is my mother,
and who are my brothers?"

And stretching out his hand
toward his disciples, he said,
"Here are my mother and my brothers!

For whoever does the will
of my Father in heaven
is my brother,
and sister, and mother."
Matthew 12:46-50

Let your manner of life
be worthy
of the gospel of Christ.
Philippians 1:27

The common bond
of godly people
is good will.
Proverbs 14:9
(Living Bible)

Let us choose
what is right;
let us determine among ourselves
what is good.
Job 34:4

I delight to do thy will,
O my God;
thy law
is within my heart.
Psalms 40:8

Look at the ships also;
though they are so great
and are driven by strong winds,

they are guided
by a very small rudder
wherever the will
of the pilot directs.
James 3:4

One ship drives east, and another west
With the self-same winds that blow:
'Tis the set of the sails
and not the gales,
Which decides the way we go.

Like the winds of the sea
are the ways of fate,
As they voyage along through life;
'Tis the will of the soul
That decides its goal,
And not the calm or the strife.

Ella Wheeler Wilcox

MY COVENANT WITH GOD

I acknowledge God as the source of my good & ask my Higher Power to guide me as I list the goals and desires I believe necessary for a successful, happy life. **I ASK GOD TO HELP ME ACHIEVE**

_____

_____

In return for God fulfilling these needs, I agree to give an equivalent measure of myself in time, energy, money, and service to God and to the people around me. **Specific actions I will immediately take in gratitude for the good I have requested are**

_____

_____

Signature: _____ **Date:** _____

I TAKE CHARGE OF MY LIFE BY SETTING
SPECIFIC GOALS.

EACH NEW DECISION I MAKE TODAY BECOMES A
NEW REALITY IN MY LIFE TOMORROW.

I RISE TO THE HEIGHT OF MY GOALS!

I CHOOSE THE HIGHEST AND BEST FOR ALL
CONCERNED.

EVERYBODY WINS!

I DEDICATE MYSELF TO BE OF MAXIMUM
SERVICE TO GOD AND MY FELLOW MAN,

TO LIVE IN A MANNER THAT WILL SET THE
HIGHEST EXAMPLE FOR OTHERS TO FOLLOW, AND
TO REMAIN AN OPEN CHANNEL OF GOD'S WILL!
(Jack Boland)

DIVINE ORDER

**I circulate God's good and
I am in all ways prospered.**

COSMOS

Divine Order is the harmony, flow, serendipity, success, and beauty I experience when I put God first in my life and practice spiritual laws and principles.

I live in an orderly universe. God's universe is a cosmos, not a chaos. The movement of the planets in their orbits, the balance of nature, the growth and unfoldment of every living thing - all reflect God's handiwork and order. When I am in tune with God, my life is orderly too!

I give thanks for the order in my world. God has created a world of unceasing beauty and order. Flowers and trees, lakes and streams, clouds and stars - every aspect of the beauty and order in my world is a cause for celebration. Divine Order manifests itself in nature, and I delight in the wonders of the world around me. I continually marvel at the glorious harmony that is everywhere present. I am awed by radiant sunsets and by countless stars shimmering in the sky.

I live in eternity now. I have all

the time I need. I schedule my time
wisely and accomplish more with less
effort. My tasks are completed with
poise and serenity. I have the ability
to do all things in order and on time.

I function as a unique individual in
a divinely ordered world. Each new day
brings opportunities for me to share my
blessings with others. I have something
valuable to contribute to the world. As
I share my blessings, I find that they
return to me increased and multiplied. I
give generously, and I receive grate-
fully. I give of my time, talents, and
resources. As I give generously to bless
others, I attract abundant good to me.

SYMBOLS OF DIVINE ORDER

Old Testament - Elisha

Elisha created order wherever he went. He multiplied oil for a widow so she could pay her debts, healed leprosy, and raised a boy from the dead. When the desert army feared death from lack of water, he correctly predicted the Lord would "make this dry stream-bed full of pools." He multiplied a few barley loaves to feed one hundred hungry prophets.

New Testament - James, Son of Alphaeus

James was selected from a large company of followers for special training as part of the inner circle of twelve disciples. Jesus taught James through question and answer, discussion, and memorization. James was then sent out to preach the coming of the kingdom, cast out demons, and heal diseases.

Color - Olive Green
Stone - Topaz

WHEN YOUR SHIP COMES IN,

YOUR RELATIVES
WILL BE WAITING ON THE DOCK.

****

They shall eat the fruit
of their way.
Proverbs 1:31

He who had received the five talents came
forward, bringing five talents more, saying
"Master, you delivered to me five talents;
here I have made five talents more."

His master said to him, "Well done, good
and faithful servant; you have been faithful
over a little, I will set you over much;
enter into the joy of your master."
Matthew 25:20-21

But remember this - if you give little,
you will get little. A farmer who plants
just a few seeds, will get only a small
crop, but if he plants much, he will reap
much. Every one must make up his own mind
as to how much he should give. Don't force
anyone to give more than   he really wants
to, for cheerful givers are the ones God
prizes. God is able to make it up to you
by giving you everything you need and more,
so that there will not only be enough for
your own needs, but plenty left over to
give joyfully to others.
2 Corinthians 9:6-8
(Living Bible)

A man's gift makes room for him
and brings him before great men.
Proverbs 18:16

It is possible to give away and become
richer! It is also possible to hold on
too tightly and lose everything.

Yes, the liberal man shall be rich! By
watering others, he waters himself.
Proverbs 11:24-25
(Living Bible)

WRITE IT DOWN

One of the greatest tools for organizing your life is simply paper and pen. Carry them with you wherever you go and whenever you get an inspired thought or idea, write it down. Once you write it down, your mind becomes free to think about other creative ideas instead of trying to remember the old ones.

When entering high school, I was required to choose a major. Being from a farm, but intending to go to college, I took two majors - college prep and vocational agriculture. The classes were fun and exciting but I had no room in my schedule for study halls.

Out of necessity I wrote daily lists of what I needed to do and became very organized and time efficient. Whenever the teacher was not talking, I would be doing homework for that class or another one. I did homework on the school bus and while lifting eggs onto the egg washer conveyor.

These habits helped me a lot in Veterinary School where I carried 24 credit hours per semester for four years. Lectures and labs ran from 8AM to 5PM with only short breaks and lunch. Because I reviewed notes at lunch and during short breaks between classes, I was able to relax and play more after school was out and keep my emotional sanity as well.

DIVINE ORDER LIST

List areas of your life in which you would like God to help you create more flow, harmony, and order.

1. _____

2. _____

3. _____

4. _____

5. _____

6. _____

7. _____

8. _____

9. _____

Wealth brings many new friends...
Many seek the favor of a generous man,
and every one is a friend
to a man who gives gifts.
Proverbs 19:4,6

If you give, you will get! Your gift will
return to you in full and overflowing
measure, pressed down, shaken together
to make room for more, and running over.

Whatever measure you use to give - large
or small - will be used to measure what
is given back to you.
Luke 6:38
(Living Bible)

Each tree is known by its own fruit.

For figs are not gathered from thorns,
nor are grapes picked from a bramble bush.
The good man out of the good treasure
of his heart produces good.
Luke 6:44-45

May there be peace
within your walls

and prosperity
in your palaces.
Psalms 122:7
(Living Bible)

Blessed is the man who...
his delight is in the law of the LORD,
and on his law he meditates day and night.

He is like a tree
planted by streams of water,
that yields its fruit in its season,
and its leaf does not wither.

In all that he does, he prospers.
Psalms 1

The abundance of the sea shall be turned
to you, the wealth of nations shall come
to you.
A multitude of camels shall cover you up
...They shall bring gold and frankincense,
and shall proclaim the praise of the LORD.
Isaiah 60:5-6

The Lord said to Moses,
"Look, I'm going to rain
down food from heaven...

That evening vast numbers
of quail arrived
and covered the camp

... and when the dew disappeared...
it left tiny flakes
of something as small as hoarfrost
on the ground...

And the food became known as
"manna"

(meaning "What is it?")
Exodus 16:4-31
(Living Bible)

Before they call
I will answer,

while they are yet speaking
I will hear.
Isaiah 65:24

Honor the LORD
with your substance
and with the first fruits
of all your produce;
then your barns will be filled
with plenty,
and your vats will be bursting
with wine.
Proverbs 3:9-10

Bring all the tithes
into the storehouse
so that there will be food enough
in my Temple;
if you do,
I will open up
the windows of heaven
for you
and pour out a blessing so great
you won't have room
enough to take it in!

Try it!
Let me prove it to you!
Your crops will be large...
And all nations
will call you blessed,
for you will be
a land sparkling with happiness.
Malachi 3:10-12
(Living Bible)

The purpose of tithing

is to teach you always
to put God first
in your lives.

Deuteronomy 14:23
(Living Bible)

I AM A PRINCE OF SERENDIPITY!

I AM ALWAYS IN THE RIGHT PLACE AT THE
RIGHT TIME.

I ORDER MY LIFE THROUGH MY VIBRATIONS!

I GET WHAT I WANT BY HELPING ENOUGH OTHER
PEOPLE GET WHAT THEY WANT.

ALL THAT I GIVE FREELY, COMES BACK TO ME
MULTILPLIED, HEAPED UP, PRESSED DOWN,
AND RUNNING OVER!

I CREATE BEAUTY, JOY, HEALTH, HAPPINESS,
AND MORE MONEY WITH MY MONEY!

I AM RICH, WELL, AND HAPPY IN EVERY PHASE
OF MY LIFE NOW!

ZEAL

**I have boundless energy!
I feel good!**

THE POWER OF PASSION

Zeal is my God-given power for sustained, enthusiastic action to do the things that need to be done by me. Through enthusiasm and persistence I can solve any problem and overcome any obstacle.

I awaken each morning with abundant energy, ready and eager to go into action. My joy and enthusiasm add new spark and determination and give greater meaning to all areas of my life.

Inspiration is everywhere in life, and I need to recognize it. Whatever strikes a special chord of awareness within me will prompt greater accomplishments. I regularly attend activities that inspire me to greater accomplishment. Loved ones motivate me in conversation and acts. Special trips and beautiful days are greatly moving.

The key to finding inspiration and motivation is my awareness. I take time to notice my many blessings along the road of life. I choose to wake up with a song of rejoicing in my heart and take that song with me throughout my day. Gratitude for special blessings, inspires

me to look further & discover even more
good in my life.

As I am inspired, I am also
inspiring to others. Everything I say
and do is uplifting. Joy permeates my
mind and body, and my whole world is
blessed and transformed. I have a zest
for living. I radiate happiness and good
cheer wherever I am, wherever I go. I
pursue my dreams with intensity,
enthusiasm, and excellence.

SYMBOLS OF ZEAL

Old Testament - Jacob

Jacob's enthusiasm for God began when he had his famous dream of a ladder to heaven with angels ascending and descending. He wrestled all night with an angel and refused to let it go until the angel had blessed him. The angel dubbed him Israel. Jacob worked fourteen years to earn his two wives and his twelve sons founded the twelve tribes of Israel.

New Testament - Simon, the Zealot

The disciple Simon was a member of the Zealots who considered themselves the agents of God to deliver Israel from foreign oppressors. Their banner was "No rule but the Law - No King but God." At the feeding of the five thousand, the Zealots wished to make Jesus King.

Color - Orange
Stone - Chrysoprase

THE GREATEST OAK

WAS ONCE A LITTLE NUT
THAT HELD ITS GROUND.

****

Never lag in zeal
and in earnest endeavor;

be aglow
and burning with the Spirit,
serving the Lord.
Romans 12:11
(Amplified Bible)

Moses didn't realize
as he came back down the mountain
with the tablets
that his face glowed
from being in the presence of God.

Because of this radiance
upon his face,
Aaron and the people of Israel
were afraid to come near him...

When Moses had finished speaking with them,
he put a veil over his face,

but whenever he went
into the Tabernacle
to speak with the Lord,
he removed the veil
until he came out again;

then he would pass on to the people
whatever instructions God had given him,

and the people would see
his face aglow.
Exodus 34:29-35
(Living Bible)

You shall receive power

when the Holy Spirit
has come upon you.
Acts 1:8

HAVE FUN!

Having an abundant life means not only being a survivor, but also being an overcomer who lives life with joy and enthusiasm. The Boy Scouts of America teaches not only crafts and survival skills but more importantly a postitve attitude to the minds of young boys. One of these attitudes I learned in scouts was zeal and enthusiasm. Whatever Troop 8 took on, we did it with all our hearts. At the end of a twenty-two mile hike we celebrated by sprinting to the end and doing cartwheels. During the mile swim event at summer camp one of our members chose to do two underwater summersaults each lap at the deep end.

One snowy winter weekend we back-packed into a local woods through twelve inches of snow for our annual Polar Bear campout. We not only survived, we did it with style and had a great time! We pitched our tents ourselves, built camp-fires, cooked hobo dinners in aluminum foil and sang songs. We were as snug as bugs in rugs in our toasty sleeping bags. The quality of our weekend was not dictated by the weather. Our spirit of joy and enthusiasm guaranteed us fun and adventure under all conditions.

You shall see
and be radiant,

your heart shall thrill
and rejoice.
Isaiah 60:5

The people of Israel
celebrated the Passover at Jerusalem
for seven days with great joy.

... the Levites and priests
praised the Lord
with music and cymbals
day after day.

... The enthusiasm continued,
so it was unanimously decided
to continue the observance
for another seven days.

... Then the people of Judah ...
were filled
with deep joy.
2 Chronicles 30:21-25
(Living Bible)

Clap your hands,
all peoples!

Shout to God
with loud songs of joy!
Psalms 47:1

It was this enthusiasm
of yours

that stirred up
many of them
to begin helping.
2 Corinthians 9:2
(Living Bible)

My zeal for God
and his work

burns hot within me...
For now is the time.
Psalms 69:9,13
(Living Bible)

I serve
with all my spirit...

I am willing
and eagerly ready.
1 Romans 1:9,15
(Amplified Bible)

The disciples
were continually diffused
(throughout their souls)
with joy
and the Holy Spirit.
Acts 13:52
(Amplified Bible)

Not by might,
nor by power,

but by my Spirit,
says the Lord of Hosts -
you will succeed
because of my spirit.
Zechariah 4:6
(Living Bible)

I SIZZLE WITH ZEAL AND ENTHUSIASM THAT
SPURS ME ON TO GREAT ACCOMPLISHMENTS.

I AWAKEN EACH MORNING WITH ABUNDANT
ENERGY, READY AND EAGER TO GO INTO
ACTION.

I FEEL GOOD! I FEEL GREAT!

JOY AND ENTHUSIASM BRING COLOR AND
SPARKLE INTO MY WORLD.

I AM AN IRRESISTABLE MAGNET FOR POSITIVE
PEOPLE AND EXPERIENCES.

MY ATTITUDE IS CONTAGIOUS!

I ELECTRIFY MY WORLD AS I GO FORTH
ACHIEVING MY EVERY GOAL!

RENUNCIATION

**I am free to accept and enjoy all the
wonderful things life has in store for me.**

WHEN ONE DOOR CLOSES,
ANOTHER DOOR OPENS

Renunciation is my mind's power to
say no to what I do not want or what is
not good for me. Renunciation erases and
eliminates self-defeating beliefs and
situations. As I renounce the old, God
creates the new.

Light is essential to growth and
strength. When a plant is moved from a
dark corner to a place of light, it grows
and flourishes. Its branches are
strengthened, the foliage turns a darker
green, and new leaves appear. Likewise,
a mind that is in the shadow of worry and
anxiety is transformed when it is exposed
to the light of God. Through my power of
Renunciation, I say "no" to negative
thoughts and unhappy feelings. I value
the eraser that exists in my mind, the
capacity to say no. I will not feel
negative emotional responses to my life.
I erase them. I make a vacuum for the
positive to come in!

I am free from judgment and
criticism under the guise of helping "to
fix." I love, inspire, and encourage -
mine is not to change anyone except
myself. I easily forgive others as I

behold the Christ in them. When I behold
the Christ in others, I know that they
are unfolding spiritually at their own
pace. Then I find it easier to look past
seeming mistakes and shortcomings to the
great qualities that are yet to unfold.

I regard all people as they truly
are - expressions of God. I focus on
their special qualities and potential for
expressing good. I realize that another
person's actions cannot keep me from my
good; however, my reactions certainly
can. I forgive, forget, and let go as I
behold the greater good in each person.
I also forgive and release myself
for any mistakes I may have made. I
release the past and step forward into
the future. Forgiveness allows me to live
in the present moment and to enjoy the
blessings of life right now. I am
transformed by the renewing of my mind.
Just as blossoms burst forth in an array
of brilliance and freedom, I, too, am
free to move ahead and leave behind old
limitations and habits. I am open and
receptive to new ideas and new experiences. I am free to accept and enjoy all
the wonderful things life has in store
for me.

SYMBOLS OF RENUNCIATION

Old Testament - Moses

Moses lead the Exodus of the Israelites from slavery and oppression, through wilderness and tribulations, to the Promised Land. Throughout the many adversities he overcame Moses often went to a quiet place in a tent or on a mountain to speak to God "face-to face".

New Testament - Thaddaeus

At the Last Supper Thaddaeus (Judas, not Iscariot) asked, "Lord, how is it that You will reveal Yourself - make Yourself real - to us and not to the world?" Jesus answered "..the Comforter ... the Holy Spirit, Whom the Father will send in My name-in My place to represent Me and act on My behalf, He will teach you all things." John 14:22-26
(Amplified New Testament)

Color - Russet
Stone - Jacinth

GOOD TO FORGIVE,
BEST TO FORGET.

HE WHO SLINGS MUD
GENERALLY LOSES GROUND.

****

Repent

- that is think differently;
change your mind,
regretting your sins
and changing your conduct

- for the kingdom of heaven
is at hand.
Matthew 3:2
(Amplified Bible)

Remember not the former things,
nor consider the things of old.

Behold, I am doing a new thing;
now it springs forth.
Isaiah 43:18-19

"Flee for your lives,"
the angels told him.
"And don't look back.

Escape to the mountains..."
But Lot's wife looked back...
and became a pillar of salt.
Genesis 19:17,26
(Living Bible)

For freedom
Christ has set us free.
Galatians 5:1

Forgive us our debts,

As we also
have forgiven our debtors.
Matthew 6:12

LETTING GO

Negative emotions are normal responses to events in our lives. The big three are anger, fear, and grief. All other negative emotions may be placed under one of these groups. Our goal is not to stuff these feelings, but to process and release them so we can live healthy, happy, and productive lives.

Shortly after I graduated from veterinary school, I received a call from the farm in Ohio. My baby brother Clay- twelve years old - had been hit by a car and was in critical condition. Clay was in the middle of the road proudly displaying his new moped to a neighbor when a car came unexpectedly over the hill and sent him flying like a ragdoll into the next neighbor's yard.

The family and I kept vigil at the hospital. After a coma of several days and two surgeries, Clay died. Each family member dealt with their grief in their own personal way. My next older brother, Cory, climbed to the very top of the tall pine tree in the front yard where he and Clay had hung lights last Christmas. I climbed into the barn attic to be alone.

My sister Lucy maintained a cheerful facade and Lily wrote a eulogy for the newspaper. Dad was initially angry and wished to sue the driver. Mom didn't eat and became alarmingly thin for several months. She collected all Clay's pictures and put them up everywhere and in a scrapbook.

At Clay's memorial the emergency room staff stopped by and Dad thanked them publicly for the excellent care they had given his baby boy.

MY RENUNCIATION LIST

I forgive and release the following

Angers: _____

_____

Fears: _____

_____

Griefs: _____

_____

If you forgive men their trespasses,

> your heavenly Father
> also will forgive you.
> Matthew 6:14

I will forgive their iniquity,

> and I will remember
> their sin no more.
> Jeremiah 31:34

Put your sword back into its place,

> for all who draw the sword
> will die by the sword.
> Matthew 26:52
> (Amplified Bible)

> They shall beat their swords into
> plowshares, and their spears into
> pruning hooks;
> nation shall not lift up sword against
> nation, neither shall they learn war
> any more.
> Micah 4:3

I have swept away your transgressions
like a cloud,
and your sins like mist;
return to me, for I have redeemed you.
Isaiah 44:22

I forgave you
all that debt
because you besought me;

and should not you
have had mercy
on your fellow servant,
as I had mercy on you?
Mat 18:32-33

Don't criticize,
and then you won't be criticized!
For others will treat you
as you treat them.

And why worry about a speck
in the eye of a brother
when you have a board in your own?
... First get rid of the board.
Then you can see
to help your brother.
Matthew 7:1-5
(Living Bible)

Let him who is without sin
among you

be the first
to throw a stone.
John 8:7

Judge not,
and you will not be judged;

condemn not,
and you will not be condemned;

forgive,
and you will be forgiven.
Luke 6:37

Be not quick to anger,

for anger lodges
in the bosom of fools.
Ecclesiastes 7:9

The disciples came and said to him,

"Do you know
that the Pharisees were offended
when they heard this saying?"

He answered, "...Let them alone;
they are blind guides.

And if a blind man
leads a blind man,
both will fall into a pit."
Matthew 15:12-14

A fool gives full vent
to his anger,

but a wise man
quietly holds it back.
Proverbs 29:11

Do not let the sun go down
on your anger.
Ephesians 4:26

Do not give dogs
what is holy;

and do not throw
your pearls before swine,

lest they trample them under foot
and turn to attach you.
Matthew 7:6

"Don't worry about a thing,"
David told him.
"I'll take care of this Philistine!

...The Lord who saved me
from the claws and teeth
of the lion and bear
will save me!"

... As Goliath approached,
David ran out to meet him.
1 Samuel 17:32-48
(Living Bible)

Don't worry about "things"
- food, drink, money, and clothes.
For you already have life
and a body
- and they are far more important
than what to eat and wear.
Look at the birds!
They don't worry
about what to eat
- they don't need to sow or reap
or store up food
- for your heavenly Father
feeds them.
And you are far more valuable to Him
than they are.
Will all your worries
add a single moment
to your life?
And why worry about your clothes?
Look at the field lilies!
They don't worry about theirs.
Yet King Solomon in all his glory
was not clothed
as beautifully as they.
And if God cares so wonderfully
for flowers that
are here today
and gone tomorrow,
won't He more surely
care for you?
... So don't be anxious
about tomorrow.
God will take care
of your tomorrow too.
Live one day at a time.
Matthew 6:25-34
(Living Bible)

****

As the Sunday School teacher
was describing how Lot's wife
looked back and
turned into a pillar of salt,

little Norman interrupted.

"My mother looked back once
while she was driving,"

he announced triumphantly,

"and she turned into
a telephone pole!"

****

I ERASE AND ELIMINATE ALL SELF - DEFEATING THOUGHTS, FEELINGS, AND SITUATIONS!

I FORGIVE MYSELF FOR ALL MISTAKES I HAVE MADE.

I FORGIVE AND RELEASE EVERYONE WHO HAS INJURED OR HARMED ME IN ANY WAY.

MY MISTAKES ARE FORGIVEN AND CANCELLED BECAUSE I FORGIVE AND ERASE THE MISTAKES OF ALL OTHER PERSONS.

I RELEASE EVERYTHING AND EVERYONE THAT IS NOT FOR MY HIGHEST GOOD.

I MAKE A VACUUM FOR THE POSITIVE TO COME IN!

I MAKE WAY FOR NEW IDEAS, NEW ACTIVITIES, AND NEW RELATIONSHIPS!

LIFE

My life is a miracle in the making.

THE SECOND COMING OF CHRIST

Life is the Holy Spirit (the whole spirit of God), active within me, renewing my body, mind, and spirit, through growth, transformation, and positive change.

I enter into the flow of life as I recognize and accept change as a part of life. Without change, my life stagnates. God is always with me, even in the midst of change. Life is constantly changing, and my part is to be open and receptive to the flow of God's good in my life.

I welcome opportunities to discover new blessings. Every new event that change brings is filled with potential, and I have a new opportunity to develop that potential. I can exceed old limits through new accomplishments. I accept new events with openness & willingness. Each change offers me the possibility of greater good.

I am changed as my awareness of my Christ within unfolds. In this unfoldment, I give greater expression to the Christ and to my true spiritual nature. Christ is born anew in me. I am healed and made whole in mind and body. The

Christ spirit within is my source of
eternal life and dynamic energy. My body
is alive and aglow with the radiant
Christ spirit and shows forth increased
vitality, health, and wholeness. The
perfect life of God flows in and through
me as a continuous healing stream.

I show forth the splendor of God
that is within me. A bulb, like a seed,
contains within itself the pattern and
elements that produce the flowering
plant. Likewise, God created within me
the splendor to produce a full, flowering
life.

I manifest my own God-given
qualities just as completely as the lily.
From my glorious God center within, I
spread joyfulness through my activities
to everyone I meet. I surround myself
with unfolding harmony as pleasing as
the fragrant aroma of the lily. The lily
does not end when the bulb has finished
blooming. Resting for a season, the lily
comes to life anew. After each night's
sleep, I awaken to the promise inherent
in every day. Daily, through the
awakening of fresh ideas, the reforming
of thoughts, and the realignment of
attitudes, I express the resurrection of
life.

I live in the eternal now. Life can
only be lived in the now of time, not at
some future date and time. This is the
day that the Lord has made and I rejoice
and am glad in it. I look for and find
the good that is present in this moment.
My life is a miracle in the making!

SYMBOLS OF LIFE

Old Testament - Noah

Noah prepared for the Great Flood (symbolic of life's adversities) by building an Ark (positive spiritual consciousness) according to God's specifications. After surviving the flood, Noah gave thanks to God and God responded, setting a rainbow in the sky as a sign that Noah would be successful and prosper.

New Testament - Matthias

Matthias was the thirteenth apostle and selected to replace Judas. Matthias followed Jesus from baptism to crucifixtion and from resurrection to ascention. He was one of seventy sent out two by two early in Jesus' ministry. Matthias' name means "given wholly unto God."

Color - Red
Stone - Amethyst

ETERNAL LIFE

Eternal life means more than endless life. It means a rich meaningful life that seems timeless because you are always living and enjoying the present moment. It is the genuine or true life that results from practicing spiritual principles and dedicating your life to good (God).

According to the Bible, all people will have an endless duration of life, either in the blessing of God's presence, or in the "hell" of God's absence. The thing that distinguishes the life of these two groups of people is not its duration, but its quality.

By practicing the principles of the Twelve Powers you create for yourself the full, beautiful life for which your heart yearns. Within you lies a wonderful potential ready to blossom forth. The life God has given you is a precious gift. Through the Christ spirit within you, your life can become a fountain of miraculous demonstrations.

THE SKY'S THE LIMIT,

BUT WE EARN OUR WINGS
EVERYDAY.

****

Be constantly renewed
in the spirit of your mind -
having a fresh mental
and spiritual attitude;

And put on the new nature
(the regenerate self)
created in God's image.
Ephesians 4:23-24
(Amplified Bible)

Nicodemus said to him,
"How can a man be born
when he is old?
Can he enter a second time
into his mother's womb and be born?"

Jesus answered, "Truly, truly,
I say to you, unless
one is born of water and the Spirit,
he cannot enter the kingdom of God.
That which is born of flesh is flesh,
and that which is born
of the Spirit is spirit.
John 3:4-6

If any one is in Christ,
he is a new creation;

the old has passed away,
behold the new has come.
2 Corinthians 5:17

Arise, shine;
for your light has come,

and the glory of the LORD
has risen upon you.
Isaiah 60:1

BOUNCE BACK POWER

Adversity and problems are normal consequences of every day living. The important thing is not that we have problems, but is how we respond to our challenges. In 1983 Janice developed Chronic Fatigue Syndrome. She was very sensitive to formaldehye fumes, plastics, synthetics, perfumes and polyesters. She had to quit her nursing position and became housebound. She could only wear cotton and we removed all the rugs and linoleum from the house. We could not have company because Janice would get acute headaches and dizzy spells if visitors wore hair spray or perfumes. Many foods caused reactions and Janice lost a lot of weight. I thought she was dying.

Conventional doctors did not recognize Janice's syndrome in those days and therefore declared her not to be sick and she was ineligible for unemployment benefits. Janice turned to holistic doctors, became vegetarian, took chinese herbs, juiced vegetables and fruits, and began to meditate regularly. During her slow recovery, Janice learned of many

other people who had nearly identical
symptoms. Now Janice helps other people
with their recoveries through nutritional
counseling and classes on healing and
meditation.

MY FITNESS PROGRAM

Steps I will take to support
my excellent health

Healthy food choices:

_____

_____

_____

Exercise plan:

_____

_____

_____

Other changes:

_____

Her name is no longer "Sarai"
but "Sarah" ("Princess")...

I will bless her richly,
and make her
the mother of nations.

Many kings
shall be among
your posterity.
Genesis 17:15-16
(Living Bible)

****

**Today my old skin
has become as dust.**

**I will walk tall
among men
and they will
know me not,**

**for today
I am a new man,
with a new life.**

****

```
              *
          *       *
        *             *
       *               *
      *                 *
     *     LIFE     *
     *                 *
      *                 *
       *               *
        *             *
          *       *
              *
```

****
*   *
*   *
*   Life is no brief candle   *
*   to me.   *
*   *
*   It is a   *
*   sort of splendid torch   *
*   which I have got hold of *
*   for the moment,   *
*   *
*   and I want   *
*   to make it burn   *
*   as brightly as possible   *
*   *
*   before handing it on   *
*   to future generations.   *
*   *
*   George Bernard Shaw   *
*   *
*   *
****

You are the light of the world.
A city set on a hill cannot be hid.

Nor do men light a lamp and put it
under a bushel,
but on a stand,
and it gives light to all in the house.

Let your light so shine before men,
that they may see your good works
and give glory to your Father
who is in heaven.
Matthew 5:14-16

I am the light of the world;
he who follows me
will not walk in darkness,
but will have
the light of life.
John 8:12

The path of the righteous
is like the light of dawn,
which shines brighter and brighter
until full day.
Prov 4:18

The lame man
will leap up
like a deer,
and those who could not speak
will shout and sing!

Springs will burst forth
in the wilderness,
and streams in the desert.
Isaiah 35:6
(Living Bible)

The pastures will turn green again.
The trees will bear their fruit;
the fig trees and grape vines
will flourish once more...

The threshing floors
will pile high again with wheat,
and the presses overflow
with olive oil and wine.

And I will give you back
the crops the locusts ate!
Joel 3:22-25
(Living Bible)

What you have learned and received
and heard and seen in me, do.
Philippians 4:9

****

It is not the critic who counts;
not the man who points out
how the strong man stumbled,
or where the doer of deeds
could have done better.

**The credit belongs to the man
who is actually in the arena;**
whose face is marred by dust
and sweat and blood;

who strives valiantly;
who errs
and comes short again and again;
who knows the great enthusiasms,
the great devotions,
and spends himself in a worthy cause;

who at the best
knows in the end
the triumph of high achievement;
and who at the worst,
if he fails,
at least fails while daring greatly;

so that his place shall never be
with those cold and timid souls
who know neither
victory nor defeat.

Theodore Roosevelt

****

Being no hearer that forgets
but a doer that acts,

he shall be blessed
in his doing.
James 1:25

For I have given you an example,

that you also should do as I have
done to you.
John 13:15

I came
that they may have
and enjoy life,

and have it in abundance
- to the full,
til it overflows.
John 10:10
(Amplified Bible)

We glide along the tides of time
as swiftly as a racing river,
and vanish as quickly as a dream.

We are like grass
that is green in the morning
but mowed down and withered
before the evening shadows fall...

Seventy years are given us!
And some may even live to eighty...
Teach us to number our days
and recognize how few they are;
help us to spend them as we should.

O Jehovah, come and bless us!
... Satisfy us in our earliest youth
with your lovingkindness,
giving us constant joy
to the end of our lives.
Psalms 90:6-14
(Living Bible)

The water I give them...
becomes a perpetual spring
within them,
watering them forever
with eternal life.
John 4:14
(Living Bible)

The person whose ears are open
to My words

- who listens to my message -

and believes and trusts in
and clings to and relies on
Him Who sent Me

has (possesses now) eternal life.

John 5:24
(Amplified Bible)

SALUTATION TO THE DAWN

Look to this day,
for it is Life,
Within its brief span,
lie all the Verities,
and realities
of your existence.

The Bliss of Growth.
The Glory of Action.
The Splendor of Beauty.

For yesterday is but a Dream
and tomorrow is but a Vision

but today well lived
makes every Yesterday
a dream of happiness
and every tomorrow
a vision of Hope.

Look well therefore
to this day.

The Sanskrit

I BLOSSOM!

I RADIATE ABUNDANT HEALTH.

I HAVE A SPARKLE IN MY EYE, A SMILE ON MY FACE, AND A SONG IN MY HEART.

I LET MY LIGHT SHINE!

AS I MOVE THROUGH THIS DAY, I WILL SPARKLE LIKE A COMET MOVING THROUGH THE SKY.

I MOVE SWIFTLY INTO THE EXCITING LIFE I HAVE ALWAYS DREAMED OF.

CHRIST IS RISEN WITHIN ME!

TWELVE POWERS MEDITATION

As I enter into God's consciousness, **FAITH** draws my good from the invisible into the visible and my **STRENGTH** is renewed like morning dew.

God's Infinite **WISDOM** inspires, informs, directs, and guides me and the warm light of God's **LOVE** floods my being!

I speak only positive, uplifting words of **POWER** to others.

CREATIVE IMAGINATION stretches my mind to exciting new concepts and my world expands accordingly.

I practice universal principles and **SPIRITUAL UNDERSTANDING** illumines my soul.

I am an open channel of God's **WILL**, choosing the highest and best for all concerned.

I **ORDER** my life through my vibrations, and sizzle with **ZEAL** and enthusiasm, that spurs me on to great accomplishments.

I let go of the past through my power of **RENUNCIATION**, and forgive and release everyone and everything that is not for my highest good.

I am a new creation, I rise and shine, for my light has come, my **LIFE** is abundant and eternal.

POWER CENTERS

The more you use your Super Powers the more powerful they become. A meditation tool for tapping into the Twelve Powers is the Power Centers given to Charles Fillmore in a vision in 1930.

When you desire **Love**, visualize a pink light glowing in your heart similar to E.T.'s heartlight. Allow the pink light to radiate through your body and then spread to the room, your city, all the beings of the earth, and then to the universe. Send out lots of love and feel that love returning to you multiplied tenfold.

For **Wisdom**, see yellow rays of sunshine warming your soul in your stomach area. God is sending you illumination through your intuition and gut feelings.

God also communicates to you with thoughts and ideas through your Super Power of **Creative Imagination**. Picture a sky blue light behind your eyes projecting onto the screen of your mind. Pose questions to God and see answers flash onto the screen. Other centers are:

Faith	Center brain-pineal
Strength	Lower back-adrenals
Wisdom	Solar plexus-stomach
Love	Heart
Power	Throat
Imagination	Front brain-pituitary
Understanding	Right forebrain
Will	Left forebrain
Order	Navel
Zeal	Base of brain-medulla
Renunciation	Lower abdomen-colon
Life	Generative organs

SUPER POWERS ACTION PROGRAM

Jack Boland routinely sprang out of bed at 2 AM on Sunday mornings to meditate for an hour before proceeding to write his Sunday lessons. However he frequently remarked, "You can sit and meditate in the lotus position until your hair grows out the door, but nothing will happen until you go into action".

This checklist is an **action plan** for transforming your life through the Twelve Powers. Invest one week on each power, creating a twelve week program for your spiritual growth.

WEEK 1 - FAITH

1. Print the Faith affirmations from the chapter on Faith on 3x5 cards and tape them to your bathroom mirror. Read them aloud with enthusiasm three times twice daily this week.
2. Wear something dark blue daily to remind you to trust God and expect positive outcomes.
3. Associate with positive, supportive people weekly by joining an Optimist's Club, AA group, Master Mind group, or prayer support group.
4. Study the Scripture quotations on Faith in this book and reflect on how they apply to your life.

WEEK 2 - STRENGTH

1. Post your Strength affirmations on your bathroom mirror and repeat them three times twice daily.
2. Wear spring green clothing this week.
3. Build up your energy, confidence, and endurance by starting an exercise program that you can enjoy and maintain. Consider walking, running, biking, swimming, aerobics, yoga, and sports.
4. Read Strength Scripture quotations daily and create joyous happy feelings within your inner being.

WEEK 3 - WISDOM AND GOOD JUDGMENT

1. Replace your Strength affirmations with Wisdom affirmation cards on your mirror.
2. Wear a sunshine yellow shirt and matching socks or something equally outrageous.
3. Tap into your sixth sense of intuition through daily meditation and quiet reflection.
4. Read the Scriptures on Wisdom and Good Judgment.

WEEK 4 - LOVE

1. Start each morning with affirmations of Love and set the stage for a great night's rest with evening Love affirmations.
2. Wear pink and think pink. Send pink light in your mind to those who need Love including yourself.
3. Send love and appreciation to special people in your life by sending them flowers and cards telling them how wonderful they are and how grateful you are that they are in your life.
4. Build self-esteem by creating a Victory Book. Write down all the wonderful successes and accomplishments of your life. Add to this book monthly.
5. When you read the Scriptures on Love, feel as though God is talking to you directly.

WEEK 5 - POWER OF THE SPOKEN WORD

1. Read your Power affirmations twice daily.
2. When you wear purple, think of yourself as a son or daughter of a King (God) wearing the royal colors of power (symbolic of your power to shape your life and destiny).

3. Replace negative words with positive words and avoid idle gossip and negative conversations. Don't criticize, complain, or condemn.
4. Find something positive to say and look for the good in all people and circumstances.
5. Notice the recognition of the importance of your words by Biblical writers when reading the Scripture quotations from the chapter on the Power of the Spoken Word.

WEEK 6 - CREATIVE IMAGINATION

1. Read your affirmations with conviction.
2. Wear light blue. Creative Imagination is the blueprint for your future successes.
3. Cut out pictures from magazines that reflect things you would like to accomplish or experience. If you want to go to Hawaii, cut out pictures of Hawaii from travel agency brochures. Place them on a wall, poster, or in a photo album. Use positive affirmations as captions and look at the pictures often.
4. When reviewing Scripture from the chapter on Creative Imagination, observe that the significant Biblical characters had visions and were dreamers.

WEEK 7 - SPIRITUAL UNDERSTANDING

1. Print your affirmation cards.
2. Wear gold or the color gold. Gold was one of the gifts of the Wise Men.
3. Attend a class or seminar, read a book, or listen to a cassette on self-improvement, spiritual growth or Bible study.
4. Attend a church retreat or spiritual retreat center such as the Personal Growth Institute on Lakeville Lake in Oxford, Michigan. (Phone 313-394-3200 or 313-391-1600).
5. Read the Scripture quotations on Spiritual Understanding in Chapter Seven.

WEEK 8 - WILL

1. Read your Will affirmations daily.
2. Wear silver and know God's Will is goodwill. See the silver lining around every cloud.
3. Put your life purpose in focus by filling out your Covenant with God (page 113).
4. Make a list of 101 goals.
5. Purchase and use a Master Mind Goal Achiever's Book from the Church of Today, PO Box 280, Warren, Michigan 48090. (Phone 313-758-3050).
6. Read the Scriptures on Will.

WEEK 9 - DIVINE ORDER

1. Start off a divinely ordered day with Divine Order affirmations and watch God's magic unfold.
2. Wear olive green and when making purchases, face the pretty side up (the olive green side of American paper money) which affirms "IN GOD WE TRUST."
3. Place your order with God for har-money in your life by filling out the Divine Order List on page 122.
4. Give generously to your source of spiritual good and if you have the audacity, become a tither and give one-tenth of all you produce back to God.
5. Clean a room, closet, desk or car and circulate items to others that you have not used in the last six months. Eliminate clutter. Have a garage sale.
6. Read what the Bible says about productivity and generosity in the Scripture quotations from the chapter on Divine Order.

WEEK 10 - ZEAL

1. Sing your Zeal affirmations in the shower this week.
2. Fire up your attire with a bright orange tie, scarf, or socks.
3. Be outrageous and go sky diving, white water rafting, hot air

ballooning, skiing, dancing, or actually ride the rides at an amusement park.
4. Sing in the car on the way to work and get excited about doing your job with excellence and class.
5. Learn why Moses wore a veil over his face by reading your Scripture assignment.

WEEK 11 - RENUNCIATION

1. Print your affirmations on russet (reddish-brown) paper.
2. Wear russet the color of autumn leaves. Autumn symbolizes a season in your life for letting go of old ideas and situations that no longer serve your highest good.
3. Select two major angers, fears and griefs to forgive and release. Write them down on a scrap piece of paper and then burn the paper or write them on toilet paper and flush them down the toilet. They no longer have power over you.
4. Do an ongoing personal inventory. Whenever you find your buttons being pushed out of proportion to the situation, take a look at old reaction patterns that you need to transform.
5. Read the Renunciation Scripture quotations and apply their wisdom to your every day life.

WEEK 12 - LIFE

1. Sing your affirmations to yourself in the mirror twice daily.
2. Wear bright red. The Super Power of Life is your Christmas present to yourself this week. Celebrate the Christ spirit within you.
3. Write down healthy food choices and an excercise plan and then start it this week (page 164). Consider fresh fruits and vegetables and juicing.
4. Read the Scripture quotations in the chapter on Life.

BIBLE TRIVIA

How's your Bible IQ? Try these questions on your friends, spouse, fellow Bible students or minister as well as yourself before and after reading this book. Answers are at the end of the twenty questions with page numbers from this book that give more in depth details.

1. When Jesus was baptized, what did he see?

2. Who initially conceived of a belief in only one God?

3. Who was the first Apostle to perform a miracle in the name of Jesus?

4. Whose bones did the Israelites carry with them in the Exodus?

5. Who introduced Peter to Jesus?

6. Who chose wisdom above riches and honor?

7. Who danced before the Ark of the Covenant and was Israel's favorite king?

8. Who was the disciple whom Jesus loved?

9. Who exited to heaven in a blazing chariot?

10. At the Last Supper, who asked Jesus to show them the Father?

11. Who predicted the Exodus?

12. Which disciple called Jesus "the Son of God" at their first encounter?

13. Who was a vegetarian and could read "the writing on the wall".

14. At the Last Supper, Jesus told the disciples, "I go and prepare a place for you." Which disciple asked, "How can we know the way?"

15. Which disciple hosted a great feast at his home for Jesus and recorded the sayings of Jesus?

16. Who multiplied a few barley loaves to feed one hundred prophets, healed leprosy and raised the dead?

17. Who worked fourteen years to earn his two wives and was dubbed "Israel" by an angel?

18. Whose face glowed after talking to God?

19. At the Last Supper, which disciple asked Jesus how he would reveal Himself to them and not to the world?

20. Who was the thirteenth apostle selected to replace Judas?

ANSWERS

TO BIBLE TRIVIA QUESTIONS

1. The Spirit of God - page 9
2. Abraham - page 15
3. Peter - page 15
4. Joseph's - page 21
5. his brother Andrew - page 26
6. Solomon - page 38
7. David - page 49
8. John - page 49
9. Elijah - page 62
10. Phillip - page 62
11. Joseph - page 76
12. Nathanael - page 76
13. Daniel - page 90
14. Thomas - page 90
15. Matthew - page 103
16. Elisha - page 118
17. Jacob - page 132
18. Moses - page 133
19. Thaddeus - page 143
20. Matthias - page 159

GLOSSARY

Affirmation-a positive declaration you can use to help you arrive at a "yes" position in your life.

Angel-a messenger of God. A guiding spirit or influence.

Christ-is the spirit of God that dwells within you that empowers you to do the things Jesus did, and even greater things.

Consciousness-your soul or mind. The sum toal of your thoughts and feelings. Higher consciousness is your positive thoughts and feelings (i.e. your Twelve Powers) which put you in harmony with creation and God.

Creative Imagination-is the spiritual power of visualization that gives form to all your world. Your dreams and visions are the blueprints of your future successes.

Devil-lower consciousness (negative thoughts and feelings) which tempt you in the wilderness away from God and your good.

Divine Order-is the harmony, flow, serendipity, success, and beauty you experience when you put God first in your life and practice spiritual laws and principles.

Faith-your confident belief that God's mighty power is actively at work in every area of your life.

Feelings-subjective   responses and emotions.
Positive feelings are summarized by six
of the Twelve Powers-Strength, Wisdom
and Good Judgment, Love, Divine Order,
Renunciation, and Life.

God-is the reality of your being. He is your
Life, your Mind and Spirit, the animating
Principle, your Creator and the Substance
and Soul of your being. God is a loving
presence in the midst of you, closer than
breathing, and is found in the stillness
of my being, when thought is tranquil.

Heaven-is God's   dwelling place or Kingdom.
Because God is   omnipresent   (present
everywhere in the universe), heaven is
present within your mind when it is fo-
cused on heavenly thoughts and feelings
(i.e. your Twelve Powers).

Holy Spirit-the whole Spirit of God which de-
scends upon you like a dove when you
turn to God. Attributes of the Holy
Spirit (Counselor and Comforter) are
summarized by the Twelve Powers.

I AM-the spirit of God   residing within you.
Jesus called it "the Father" (Abba).
It is the shortened form of God's re-
sponse to Moses' request for the name
of the God of the patriarchs (I am who
I am.)

Kingdom of God (Heaven)-the central part of
Jesus' preaching. It means the rule of
God within your life. The Kingdom is at
hand in your life when you focus upon
divine ideas (i.e. the Twelve Powers),
allowing them to express as perfect harmony.

Life-is God's spirit active within you, renewing your body, mind, and spirit through growth, transformation, and positive change. Eternal life means not only endless life, but also a rich meaningful life that seems timeless because you are living in the present moment.

Love-is the spirit of God in you loving all creation. Love is a great harmonizer and healer. Love sees good everywhere and in everybody and brings out the best in them.

Mind-is your collective thoughts and feelings. In Scripture, referred to as your heart or soul.

Personality-is the mortal temporary roles, characters, and behaviors you assume between birth and biological death.

Power of the Spoken Word-the creative power that converts your spoken and unspoken thoughts and feelings into living fact.

Renunciation-your mind's power to say "no" to what you do not want or what is not good for you. Renunciation erases and eliminates self-defeating beliefs and situations.

Soul-is the immortal and eternal spiritual you that thinks, feels, makes choices, and learns from the consequences of your actions.

Spirit-the gracious personal God presence that lives within you (Holy Spirit, Comforter, Counselor, I AM, or Christ spirit) waiting to be expressed through your Super Powers of the Mind (the Twelve Powers.)

Spiritual Understanding-is your awakened a-
wareness of your spiritual nature and
heritage. Tapping into a reservoir of
divine intelligence, you gain new understanding, enlightenment, and illumination.

Strength-is your capacity for sustained conviction and joy. No adversity can destroy your optimism or turn you back
from your spiritual quest.

Super Powers of the Mind-the Twelve Powers
through which God expresses His great
good in your life: Faith, Strength, Wisdom and Good Judgment, Love, Power of
the Spoken Word, Creative Imagination,
Spiritual Understanding, Will, Divine
Order, Zeal, Renunciation, and Life.

Thoughts-are ideas and concepts that come to
you as a result of thinking, reflection,
or meditation.

Transformation-changing your life in a positive direction by turning it over to God
and practicing universal spiritual principles taught by the Bible and Jesus.

Will-is your mind's decision making power that
brings dynamic spiritual forces into play
to acheive your inspired choices and objectives.

Wisdom and Good Judgment-is your God-given
intuitive ability to clearly know the
truth and to be divinely guided and directed at all times.

Zeal-is your power for sustained, enthusiastic
action to do the things that need to be
done by you. Joy permeates your mind
and body, and you have a zest for living.

INDEX

Did You Borrow This Book?

Want a Copy of Your Own?

Need a Great Gift for a Friend or Loved One?

Your local library or bookstore
will be delighted to order your copy
from America's leading wholesaler of books:

BAKER & TAYLOR BOOKS